Rambles
in
North
Nottinghamshire

Malcolm McKenzie

Published by Sigma Leisure – an imprint of
Sigma Press, 1 South Oak Lane, Wilmslow, Cheshire SK9 6AR, England.

British Library Cataloguing in Publication Data
A CIP record for this book is available from the British Library.

ISBN: 1-85058-366-8

Typesetting and Design by: Sigma Press, Wilmslow, Cheshire.

Maps and photographs by: Malcolm McKenzie

Cover photograph: West Retford Lock, Chesterfield Canal.

Printed by: Manchester Free Press

General Disclaimer

Contents

INTRODUCTION

THE WALKS

INTRODUCTION

North Nottinghamshire is essentially a rural landscape, a peaceful area with a long and varied history. It corresponds roughly to the modern District of Bassetlaw, but even this name goes back to the Domesday book and beyond.

Walking on the Seabed

The whole of this area once formed the bed of an immense land-locked sea stretching east to Germany. A series of layers were laid down on the floor of the lake, then in the period when the Alps were formed, earth movements tipped the layers of rock eastwards.

The practical result for the walker is that in travelling from West to East, you find a series of North-South "stripes" corresponding to the under-lying rock. In the extreme West, at Shireoaks and Creswell, is the oldest layer, magnesian limestone.

The Sandlands

Further east, at Worksop and Hodsock, is a soft red sandstone, and in a wide swathe between Worksop and Retford the Bunter sandstone which is well drained and provides the driest land underfoot after wet weather. Between Retford and the Trent are clays and Keuper Marl, forming a ridge: there are always good views hereabouts. It is wisest to walk in this area after a dry spell, as the clay soil can be tenacious after a soaking.

Valleys

In the North of Nottinghamshire are the Carrs, formerly a glacial lake, then marshlands which have now been drained and converted to agriculture. The valleys of the Trent and its tributary the Idle had their share of marshes which have only been drained and the rivers tamed in relatively recent times.

Traces of Times Past

Of course, history is everywhere. One of these walks visits Creswell Crags, the former home of Neanderthal and Stone Age man. Artifacts found in the caves on either side of the gorge can be seen in the Visitor Centre. Bassetlaw was on the border between Mercia and Northumbria, whose King Edwin lost his life fighting the pagan Mercia and was buried, it is said, at Edwinstone. The sixteenth century is represented by Hodsock Priory with its Tudor gateway and the impressive Tudor Manor Lodge, to name only two.

The Pilgrim Fathers originated in Bassetlaw, and it was at Babworth church that the Separatists first met, little knowing that their future lay at nearby Scrooby, then Amsterdam, and eventually Plymouth and New England. Richard Clyfton's church also has one of the most beautiful settings in the county. See it at bluebell time.

In the West, the great estates known as the Dukeries were carved out of Sherwood Forest in the 18th century. These estates - Welbeck, Thoresby, Clumber and Worksop - still exist and some part of them all is attainable by footpath and bridleway. Clumber Park is in the safe hands of the National Trust and offers a huge variety of walks.

The Chesterfield Canal

The most valuable legacy of the past for the walker is the Chesterfield Canal, which crosses the County to join the Trent at West Stockwith. Its towpath is always a pleasure to walk, and figures in nine of the walks.

The canal was built between 1771 and 1777 to James Brindley's plans. When first constructed, it linked Chesterfield with the river Trent at

West Stockwith, a distance of 45.5 miles. The cargoes carried were coal, lead, corn, bricks and pottery, and stone quarries near the canal added to the traffic. Stone from a quarry near Anston was shipped down the canal in the 1840's to build the Houses of Parliament. The first section of the canal to be built was the Norwood tunnel, 2,890 yards long through a ridge of magnesian limestone. The collapse of this tunnel due to subsidence in 1908 meant the end of traffic above Shireoaks, and now the canal is navigable only as far as Worksop.

Towns

The "capital" of the district is Worksop, a forest settlement which has grown to a town of forty thousand inhabitants. It lays claim to being the "Gateway to the Dukeries", and has its own gateway in the gatehouse to the Priory church. Both the stately church and its unique gatehouse are worth a detour.

Only a few miles along the canal, Retford is about half the size of Worksop. It owes its prosperity to the Great North Road being diverted through the town in 1766, with the Chesterfield canal arriving in 1777.

PATHS

There must be over a thousand footpaths and bridleways in North Notts. Some could well date back to prehistory, and many owe their origins to the workaday journeys of the farmer or the horses which towed barges along the Trent and the Chesterfield canal. The area is especially rich in green lanes, leading from a village to the most distant fields or to long-abandoned fords and ferries. Some may be remnants of the old roads which kept to the high ground before marshes were drained.

LONG DISTANCE PATHS

There are two long distance paths in Nottinghamshire, the Robin Hood Way and the Trent Valley Way. The former was produced by the Nottinghamshire Wayfarers Rambling Club to link places connected to the legend of Robin Hood. The original route runs for 88 miles, but a new and longer version is in preparation. The prime mover of the path, which is described in an excellent book, was Chris Thompson, who can supply a copy if you write to him at 21 Spindle View, Calverton, Notts.

The second long distance path was published by the County Council. A book describing the Trent Valley Way, a route wandering from Thrumpton to West Stockwith and never far from the Trent itself, is accompanied by a book of nine circular walks based on the longer route. These and many

leaflets describing single walks can be obtained from the Rights of Way Officer, Trent Bridge House, Fox Road, West Bridgford, Notts.

THE WALKS

This book offers thirty-two country walks, all of them circular. The length varies from four to nine miles, and as the distribution map shows, some walks could be joined to make a longer one.

The times suggested for completing the walks allow for some leaning on a gate to look at the view, and perhaps a half-pint at one of the many village pubs.

PUBS

Most landlords welcome walkers, though they like to be warned in advance if a coach-load is arriving! However it is a matter of courtesy to take off muddy boots before rushing to the bar, or alternatively wear plastic bags over the offending boots. This keeps the carpets clean and gives the locals a laugh too.

Though pubs can now stay open all day, very few do, and rural watering holes rarely stay open beyond the old opening hours. The walk has to be timed to reach the pub between 12 and 3 approximately.

Parking

The walks usually start from some easily identifiable building, such as a church or pub. It is really vital, not just polite, to park so that no-one is obstructed, avoiding gateways and narrow lanes. Some pub landlords kindly allow walkers to use their car-parks, but please ask permission! It would be a nice gesture to have a drink after the walk and thank the landlord politely.

Travel

Most of the walks can be reached by public transport, though some villages have a fairly skimpy service. On Sundays, when most people are free to go walking, services are reduced even further.

I have tried to show what transport is available, but it is always wise to check. For up to date information, telephone Nottinghamshire County Council's bus "hotline" on Retford (0777) 710550. This service is available Monday to Friday 8am - 7pm and Saturday 8 till 1.

Maps

I hope that the walk descriptions and my sketch maps will provide enough information for accurate navigation. Of course it is always useful to have an Ordnance Survey map as well. The only practical map for checking a walking route is the Pathfinder series on a scale of 1:25,000 (2.5 inches to the mile), which shows field boundaries and quite small details. The Landranger maps at 1:50,000 are handy for finding the start of the walks.

The start of each walk is given as a map reference, a six figure number preceded by the letters SK which designate the area covered by these walks. If memories of latitude and longtitude are a little hazy, proceed as follows:-

Look along the top edge of your map for the first two figures of the map reference. When you've found them, imagine the space between this number and the next bigger divided into ten. The third figure of the map reference tells you how many tenths to measure along. From this point, imagine a line going down the map.

Next, look for the fourth and fifth figures on the edge of the map, use the sixth figure to measure tenths again, and imagine a line running from there across the map.

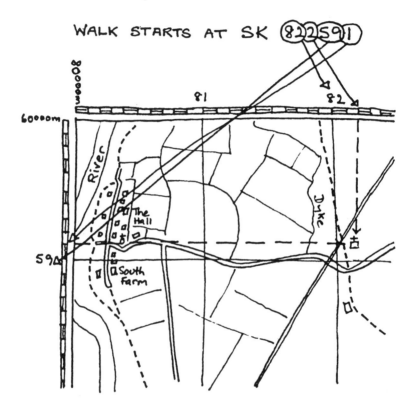

Where the two lines meet is where you want to be.

Be Prepared

It is a good idea to carry a few essentials in a light rucksack when you set out for a walk. The weather can turn nasty on the most balmy of days, so waterproofs are the first necessity. Rubberised clothing tends to make you sweat but you can get breathable fabric jackets and leggings which remain comfortable.

Something to eat and drink could come in handy: fruit is the easiest food to carry, especially in dried form, and fizzy or alcoholic drinks are less good for the thirst than fruit juice.

A small first aid kit should always be carried, with at least some sticking plasters, bandage and ointment for scratches. A compass should be unnecessary on these walks, though many experienced walkers never go without one. Finally, you might consider carrying binoculars to keep an eye on the wildlife, and if you don't bring a camera you might regret it.

Problems

The County Council's Rights of Way section has installed many new stiles and some footbridges, and have also erected signposts and way-marks to guide the walker. This has already made a large number of paths accessible which previously were not, and is greatly appreciated. Some problems may still remain, however, with illegal cropping of rights of way.

The Rights of Way Act 1990 clarified the law regarding ploughing of rights of way and made it easier for Local Authorities to deal with landowners who break the law. Headland paths - those which follow a field boundary - can not be ploughed and must be 1.5 metres wide if just a path and 3 metres if a bridleway. Cross-field paths may be ploughed, but should be clearly marked and made fit to walk on soon after ploughing. They should be one metre wide, or 1.5 metres in the case of bridleways. There should not be crops growing on them.

If crops are planted on a path and become an obstruction, Local Authorities have the right to remove the obstruction if the landowner will not, and send him the bill.

I have done all these walks at least twice. Many presented no problems at all, while some have needed stiles erecting. The problem which tends to recur, however, is that of crops blocking the path. Should you find any serious obstructions, please help by reporting them to the responsible authority. The person to write to is the Rights of Way Officer, Trent Bridge House, Fox Road, West Bridgford, Notts NG2 6BJ.

Country Code

We must never forget that people earn their living from the countryside, a tough enough job without problems caused by visitors. The Country Code is a set of rules which may seem common sense, but bear repeating here.

❏ Guard against all risk of fires

❏ Fasten all gates

❏ Keep dogs under proper control

❏ Keep to the paths across farmland

❏ Leave no litter

❏ Avoid damaging fences, hedges and walls

❏ Safeguard water supplies

❏ Protect wildlife, wild plants and trees

❏ Go carefully on country roads

❏ Respect the life of the countryside

Thanks

I would like to thank for their indispensible help in producing this book:

❏ Anne McKenzie, who has walked the walks and proofread the results, taken the photos and provided the home cooking.

❏ Margaret Dews, Tourism Officer of Bassetlaw District Council, whose advice and practical help solved so many problems.

❏ Christine Fitton, of North Notts Environmental Partnership, whose advice on matters geological added a new dimension to the countryside.

1: CLUMBER & WELBECK

A delightful woodland walk through two of the Dukeries estates, Welbeck and Clumber, with a view of Worksop Manor, another Ducal house.

Distance: 8 miles

Time: 4 hours

Start: Hannah Park Wood car park, map reference SK 591771

Maps: Pathfinders SK 47/57 (Staveley) and SK 67/77 (Clumber Park), Landranger 120 (Mansfield and Worksop)

How to Get There:

By Car: Hannah Park is just south of Worksop on the B6034

By Bus: Hourly service 32 between Mansfield and Worksop, rare buses on Sunday

Refreshments: Take a picnic

Nearest Tourist Information: Worksop Tourist Information Centre, Public Library, Memorial Avenue, Worksop (0909 501148)

Start the walk by the Lion Gate, an entrance to the Welbeck estate built for the 6th Duke of Portland in 1894. The arms of Cavendish and Bentinck are carved in stone, while the Portland arms are seen in the ironwork. Opposite is a car park created by the Woodland Trust so that visitors can enjoy the beautiful Hannah Wood.

The Woodland Trust was formed in 1972 to conserve threatened native and broad-leaved trees and woodlands, often with the help of English Nature and the Countryside Commission. Hannah Wood was saved from housing development by its intervention. The local Brownie pack did good Wombling work, clearing out the junk which intellectually disadvantaged people love to leave in beauty spots, and the wood is now carefully managed.

The entrance to the Welbeck Estate

Go almost through the car park and turn left through oak and sweet chestnut. In the network of paths, go down hill keeping within the wood not too far from the Ollerton Road. At the foot of the wood go through a slip-stile and turn right to join the road. A little further down hill cross the road to a path near the edge of the woodland opposite. At the end of the wood join the Old Coach Road and follow it ahead, with the golf course on one side and on the other Worksop College, both screened by high hedges well stocked with holly. Just beyond the College grounds a bridleway sign points to an avenue of Scots pines which skirt the playing fields. The well-used path turns half-left across two fields, then plunges into a pine forest. It is rumoured that this section will become part of a golf course, but the path itself will not be altered.

Very soon, on reaching the Forest Cottage, bear right past silver birch, then tall pine forest. On reaching a tarmac road, cross it and go a few

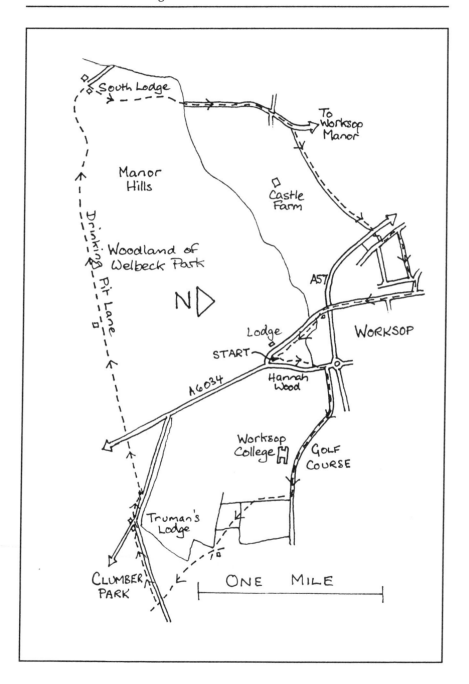

yards into Clumber Old Wood. On the right is a narrow path parallel to the road, which doubles back on itself just before Truman's Lodge. Rejoin the road here, passing a majestic beech, and pass in front of the Lodge, watching out for traffic coming through from Clumber Lane. Again, just enter the wood and turn right along a winding path which follows the road.

Very soon you will join a forest track angling away from the road. After crossing the B6034, it becomes Drinking Pit Lane, one of the few paths which cross the Welbeck estate. The woodland improves the further the lane goes: at first there are pinewoods with a narrow screen of silver birch, then a scattering of beech. Passing a neat little cottage topped by three enormous chimney-pots, we find the beech mixed with sweet chestnut; further on, brightly-painted fences and gates flank the entrance drive to Welbeck Woodhouse, a tiny lodge nestles among the trees, and majestic beech, oak and chestnut tower over the narrow lane. Finally, at a fork, our route bears left and becomes a hollow lane between low sandstone cliffs, the roots of the wayside trees forming strange shapes against the stone.

Now the path approaches a crenellated building, which from the front resembles the entrance gate to Clumber Park, except that the archway is blocked by huge wooden doors. This is one end of a tunnel built by the eccentric fifth Duke of Portland, through which he could be driven en route for Worksop. Turn right here past South Lodge, passing through mixed woodland. Beyond the wood a hedged track leads towards Worksop Manor, its sandy soil popular with rabbits. About 200 yards beyond a cross-road, climb the fence into the meadow right and follow the hedge, with only a couple of venerable, gnarled hawthorns to testify that this too was once a hedged lane. Cross stiles and steps to reach the Worksop by-pass: cross this with great care and go along a meadow to enter a pleasant housing estate.

Turn left along "Water Meadows", then right along Robinson Drive. At Sparken Hill, turn right again and walk up the hill. Recross the by-pass and after the last house on the left join a path lined with yews and oak woodland. Continue through the fine stand of beeches dominating the brow of the hill and follow the path back to the car park.

2: CRESWELL CRAGS & WHITWELL

A walk full of interest which crosses one of the Dukeries estates and skirts another. It also starts at the foremost prehistoric site in two counties, for it lies on the Notts-Derbyshire border.

Distance: 8.5 miles

Time: 4 hours

Start: Creswell Crags Visitor Centre, map reference SK 538744.

Maps: Pathfinders SK 47/57 (Staveley & Worksop) and SK 67/77 (Clumber Park), Landranger 120 (Mansfield & Worksop)

How to Get There:

By Car: The Crags are signposted 4 miles south-west of Worksop on the A60

By Bus: Service 9 Worksop-Mansfield hourly Monday to Saturday and 77 Worksop-Chesterfield hourly

Refreshments: Several pubs in Whitwell

Nearest Tourist Information: The Visitor Centre

The Creswell Crags Visitor Centre provides interpretation of the nearby limestone gorge, whose caves have revealed evidence of human and animal occupation over a period of 43,000 years, since Neanderthal Man hunted here. After the Ice Age a new breed of hunter arrived with flint tools and weapons to hunt reindeer or bison passing through the gorge. Later came Creswellian man, who could fashion rough carvings on bones subsequently found in the caves which line the gorge.

Cresswell Crags

Starting at the Visitor Centre, set off with your back to the entrance, crossing the A60 after 700 yards to enter a drive marked "Private Road". Follow the metalled road along the tree-lined drive and across fields until you cross a cattle-grid at the edge of woodland and turn left. The path follows the edge of woodlands and a sports field used by the students at the army college which now occupies Welbeck Abbey.

The Abbey was once one of the richest monastic houses in England, founded in 1153 by the "white canons" of the Premonstratensian Order. Following the Dissolution it became the home of the First Duke of Newcastle, then through marriage of the second Duke of Portland. The family made their mark, one as Prime Minister, another as a pioneer in irrigation and land management, but it was the intensely shy fifth Duke, Lord William John Cavendish-Scott-Bentinck, who expended huge sums in developing the estate, building above and below ground. An underground ballroom and several tunnels are known to exist, but cannot be visited by the general public. Though a Military College occupies some of the buildings, the estate is still owned and worked by Bentinck family.

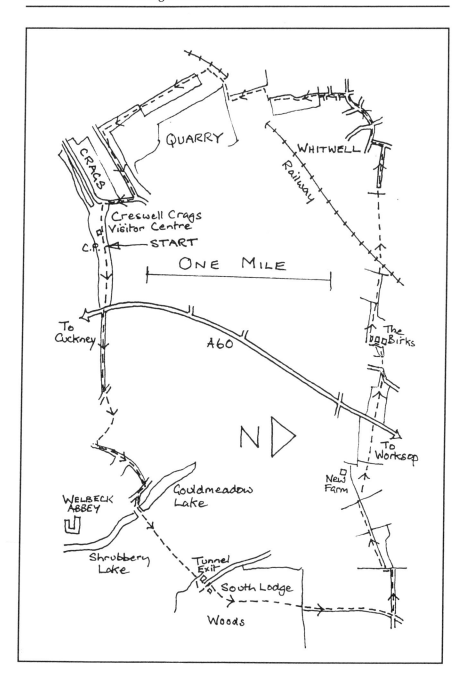

Pass through a hand-gate on to an estate road, turn right, then left after 100 yards. Turn left again to pass between two lakes, the 18th century creation of Humphrey Repton. They attract a wide variety of wild fowl, while the trees surrounding them are home to many more birds, notably herons. Walk beside a grassy strip marking the line of the tunnel built by the eccentric fifth Duke of Portland, who drove through with a carriage and four. Pass through a hand-gate and go right to some iron gates, then turn left to pass the tunnel entrance. Though the gatehouse is occupied, the tunnel itself remains closed.

Turning your back on the tunnel, go through the gate beside South Lodge signposted "Worksop 2 miles" and follow the "Tunnel Road" through the wood and on towards Worksop Manor in the distance. The Manor we see now is only a fragment of the grand design of James Paine to build the grandest private house in England. This followed a fire in 1761, which destroyed the previous 500-room Elizabethan manor. The fourth Duke of Newcastle, on buying the estate in the 19th century, pulled it down except for the service wing and courtyard.

Arriving at a crossroads, turn left along a green lane, and at the end turn left to cross a stile and go on to the end of the spinney. Turn right to cross a steam, then follow the edge of the spinney and a farm track. At the top of the hill, after passing through a gate, go through the second gap on the right and go diagonally across the field, reaching a farm track and footbridge and continuing to the A60.

Having crossed with due care, go straight up the meadow towards an electricity pole. Go through the nearby gate and straight on to another. Cross the stile beside it and approach Birks Farm along a track. A stile beside the farm gate gives access to a paddock which you cross to another stile. Now turn left past the farm buildings and right after the last one. After a stile there is a pleasant path along two meadows, the second having a stile in the corner, and through a paddock to a white gate.

After crossing a railway, your path is straight up the arable field to Whitwell, aiming for the left end of a terrace of bungalows. The path through the crops may not be exactly on this line, however. On reaching the end of Mill Lane, follow it to the end, turn left down Hanger Hill, then right at the main street. Refreshments should be easy to find as you continue through the village. After a steep hill, turn left along Franklin Avenue (opposite Jubilee Road), and at the end keep on beside a hedge. Turn right at the end, then left at a hedge end.

At this point a quarry has cut off the footpath. Turn right past Butchers Wood. This whole area, including the earthworks to the south, are a panoply of wild flowers and a constant source of interest to the walker. Go down the hill to the railway signal (on your right) and turn left across the field and walk alongside the mounds of earth. Keep ahead on a delightful path through a strip of woodland, angling left at the end to join a track. Follow it left beside varied woodland to the end, then turn right to return to the Visitor Centre. Leave time to visit the centre and stroll round the crags.

3: SHIREOAKS & RHODESIA

An intriguing walk on the Notts-Derbyshire border starts near a long-neglected Tudor mansion and passes an aristocratic Tudor hunting-lodge ready to refresh the passing traveller. And the Chesterfield canal takes you through Rhodesia!

Distance: 6 miles

Time: 3 hours

Start: Shireoaks church, grid reference SK 554809

Maps: OS Landranger 120, Pathfinders 47/57 (Staveley) and 48/58 (Kiveton Park)

How to Get There:

By Car: Shireoaks is 3 miles north-west of Worksop just off the A57

By Bus: Half-hourly services 55 and 56 from Worksop, hourly on Sundays

By Train: Shireoaks is on the Worksop/Sheffield line

Nearest Tourist Information: Worksop Tourist Information Centre, Public Library, Memorial Avenue, Worksop (0909 501148

Refreshments: Woodhouse Inn, Rhodesia, Hewett Arms, Shireoaks, Manor Lodge, Worksop

---

The Dukes of Newcastle, having sunk the first deep-mine colliery in the County here in 1845, had the church designed by local architect T.C. Hine. The foundation stone was laid by the Prince of Wales, "in the prescence of the Duke and Mr Gladstone".

Go along Thorpe Lane, which is opposite the churchyard and enter the grounds of Shireoaks Hall on the left. The path passes the old stables, which have been converted into a bright and attractive public house and

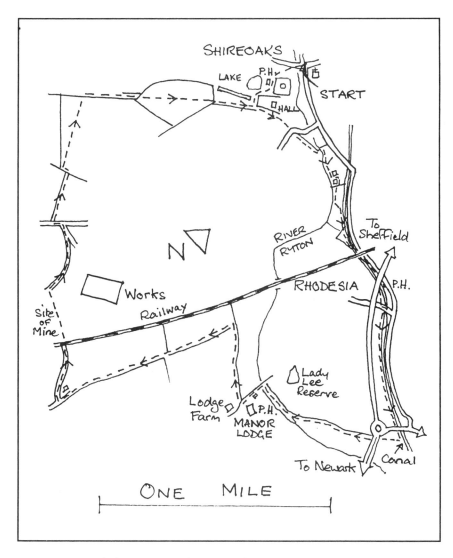

restaurant, and decorative lakes popular with fishermen. Pass between the Hall and the formal canal and turn left along a grassy sward, then the Hall drive to Spring Lane.

Cross this and follow another grass track to cross the river Ryton. In front of you the embankment of the Chesterfield Canal is just beyond the football pitch, but it can't be approached directly. Turn right past the sports club, left between it and a house and right again to circumvent the garden. After crossing a stile follow the river, then angle left to walk beside the canal bank, but only as far as a small spinney. Here climb the bank to join the tow-path, crossing the canal at a lock: take care here, there is a plank bridge over the overflow just before the obvious metal bridge. After crossing, turn right to follow the canal, in the shade of the Worksop by-pass flyover. Reaching a cul-de-sac, turn right.

This is Rhodesia, built for Shireoaks Colliery Limited to house the workers in the new mine. Naturally the canal, completed in 1777 to join Chesterfield to West Stockwith on the river Trent, was used to carry away the coal.

Cross the canal bridge and rejoin the tow-path. In spite of roads left and right, the tree-lined canal seems remote from traffic. Wall-to-wall reed mace is a reminder that no boats have ventured this far along the Chesterfield Canal since 1945: this is confirmed by the two locks we pass, where the water cascades unchecked. We pass under two bridges, then find a third beside the tow-path, a forlorn reminder of the Lady Lee branch canal which once served a quarry of that name. Turning right to pass the unused rover bridge, cross a farm road and cross the corner of the field beyond to a stile and signpost. Next you have to negotiate the two lanes of the Worksop by-pass and descend into the corner of a field.

At this point my Ordnance Survey map shows the footpath running along the middle of the field, presumably on the line of the branch canal tow-path, but in practice there is no sign of it and walkers tend to keep to the hedge-side. At the end of the field the path enters some woodland where chunks of masonry suggest long-fallen bridges and the quarry wharves. The path here runs between the River Ryton and a smaller watercourse, and winds through natural woodland. Finally it emerges on a farm-track, and Lady Lee quarry, now a Nature Reserve, is to the right.

A left turn brings you face to face with Worksop Manor Lodge. The Lodge was built for the Earl of Shrewsbury by Robert Smythson in 1593. This impressive 5-storey building lay in the demesne of Worksop Manor, which was itself built by Smythson for the Earl of Shrewsbury, fifth and last husband of the formidable Bess of Hardwick. The Manor was destroyed by fire in 1761, but the Lodge has managed to survive. It seems hard to believe, but there was once a sixth floor. The Lodge is now a public house and restaurant, which walkers should find open between 11 a.m. and 3 p.m.

Manor Lodge

Our route is to the right through a farm gate just before reaching Manor Lodge Farm. The surfaced farm track crosses a field and continues beside a high hedge: when the hedge ends, turn left to walk to the right of a hedge. On reaching a farm track, continue to the top of the hill. Pass the house and turn right along a green lane, clearly no longer used and taken over by wild flowers. At the end, there is a stile, then railway lines to be crossed.

Opposite is the site of Steetley mine: there is no trace of the buildings, and the footpath, virtually straight across, is not obvious. However, a row of bushes indicate a little-used road leading past disused quarries to a minor road. Here a board announces that the adjacent eyesore is called "Steetley Refractories Ltd". Turn left, then after 50 yards right along the edge of a field. At the end, a few steps left bring you to a path cut through the crops.

Climb the fence and turn right along a grass track. Over to the left, small aircraft swarm around Netherthorpe airfield. When the track swings left, keep straight on, through a gate and across an arable field to the far corner. Cross a stile and follow a farm track leading straight to Shireoaks Hall.

The Hall was built for Henry Hewett in 1600, probably designed by Robert Smythson. there were extensive alterations about a century later, when new stables were added and a ha-ha built at the foot of the garden. In 1811 it was partly demolished and gutted, remaining that way until the present owner began its revival.

Turning left, return past the Hewett Arms and retrace your steps to your starting point.

The Hewett Arms

4: SOUTH CARLTON & TURNERWOOD

Like many walks, this is best explored in Spring, but there is so much to see in every season that it never disappoints. There are historic buildings, several glimpses of the golfers whose fairways criss-cross Lindrick Common, and best of all my favourite stretch of the Chesterfield Canal leading down to the peaceful hamlet of Turnerwood.

Distance: 9.5 miles

Time: 5 hours

Start: South Carlton church, map reference SK 588839

Maps: Pathfinder SK 48/58 (Kiveton Park), Landranger 120 (Mansfield & Worksop)

How to Get There:

By Car: South Carlton is 3 miles north of Worksop on the A60

By Bus: Hourly services (20, 21, 22, or 24) Worksop to Doncaster, Monday to Saturday

Refreshments: No pubs on the route, unless you're a member of Lindrick Golf Club, but some idyllic sites for a picnic

Nearest Tourist Information: Worksop Tourist Information Centre, Public Library, Memorial Avenue, Worksop (0909 501148

Start at the church of Saint John the Evangelist, South Carlton. The church tower is probably the oldest in the Shire, with Saxon masonry and much early Norman work. It is also a very attractive church, beautifully maintained.

Cross the road to a gap in the wall and go through the car park provided for fishermen who are using Carlton Mill pond. Beyond this is

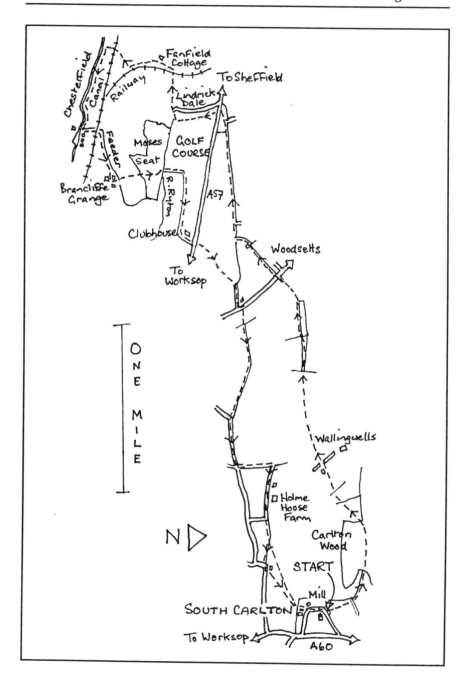

a clear path across meadowland, then around the boundary of Carlton Hall grounds to reach Carlton Wood. Carlton Hall itself was demolished in 1955 and the outbuildings subdivided.

Carlton Wood is a delightful piece of mixed woodland criss-crossed with paths, but the route is straight ahead and marked by ancient yew-trees on either side, gently bending left through rhododendrons as it nears the end of the wood. A clear path crosses three arable fields and passes between two lakes, home of the Wallingwells Angling Club.

To the right can be seen Wallingwells itself. A Benedictine nunnery was founded here in the reign of Stephen to house nine sisters and a prioress. The house fell victim to Henry VIII's nationalisation policy and had a variety of owners. The present hall was built in the late sixteenth century, though parts of the earlier structure were incorporated, and mosaic floors laid by Italian artisans about 1145 are still to be seen. When in 1927 the estate was auctioned, a builder converted the house into four separate residences.

Follow the farm-track ahead to pass between a pair of massive stone gate-posts. The dilapidated sandstone walls suggest that this was the limit of the estate or of its parkland. Next the path follows a hedged lane, a haven for wild flowers and butterflies. Where the lane widens, a "Private" sign indicates that the rest of the lane has been fenced off: the walker angles left to a bridge and follows the edge of an arable field. At the end, turn left along a track to the road, left again for 40 yards, then right at the side of a field.

Join a crushed-stone path which continues up the hill and dodges right to pass alongside the drive of Orchard Cottage. A few yards beyond is Lindrick Golf Course, an excellent test of the golfer which, because it occupies common land, has a network of footpaths crossing it. Turn right on a wide track skirting the course, with a sea of gorse on one side and a row of impressive houses on the other. Ignore a bridleway on the left, and at a fork take the wider route right, cross a track and carry on through woodland on a narrow path.

Reaching the A57, cross half-left with great care and follow a tree-lined path marked by yellow poles, then the edge of the seventh fairway. Pass the tee and the sixth green, watching out for a gap in the hedge on your right. A steep path, indicated by a signpost well hidden by blackthorn, goes down into Lindrick Dale and past a beautifully tended cottage garden. Turn left, passing on your left a long-disused quarry and on your right a thick laurel hedge. The lane swings left and passes Fanfield Cottage, which offers another delightful garden, but more unusually a door framed by a boat, plus crossed oars!

About 100 yards after crossing a bridge, turn right on a well-defined path across an arable field, cross a railway and a meadow. Before you is the Chesterfield Canal, which once carried coal and iron from Chesterfield to the Trent at West Stockwith, a journey of 46 miles. The collapse of the Norwood Tunnel in 1908, combined with competition from the railways, led to the abandonment of the 20 miles of canal to the west of Worksop. Nevertheless water still flows in this section, and the towpath is maintained for public enjoyment.

Ignore the bridge and turn left along the most beautiful stretch of this, and possibly any canal. In about half a mile, you pass 12 of the canal's 65 locks, including a "staircase" of three locks and two doubles. At the quiet waterside oasis of Turnerwood, built to serve a long-abandoned

Turnerwood

quarry, turn left at the bridge to follow the feeder canal which brings water from the river Ryton. Cross the railway again and swing right to pass a forest of foxgloves and reach a stile. Cross a grass field to reach Branclife Grange whose farm-house, and the tithe barn beside it, date from Tudor times and belonged to Roche Abbey, near Maltby.

Turn left beside the barn, cross the stone stile and climb the track to Moses Seat, a splendid beech-wood renowned for its bluebells. Drop down to cross the feeder canal for the last time, then the river Ryton by Monks Bridge. Follow the bridleway up the hill and swing right at a yellow pole to follow the edge of the golf course again. Keep to the right of the club-house to reach the A57, scuttle across and after 30 yards fork right on a grassy path through hawthorn and birch. Paths on your left go to an old quarry which has a wealth of wild flowers. Emerging on to a corner of the golf course, keep right past the 16th tee and 15th green and follow a hedged lane down to a road.

Turn left for 50 yards, then right to cross two stiles beside a farm gate. Cross a grass field and follow the farm lane which rejoins the road. Turn left for 300 yards, then left into a farm track. At the top of the hill turn right past Holme House Farm and its cottages, then pass through a gate and along a grass path. After about 100 yards a gap in the hedge should lead to a field-path to Carlton. I have never found one, so continue to the road, walk past the Lodge and cross the stile left. This field-path is well maintained and leads directly to Field House Farm. Keep to the left of the barn, emerging beside Carlton Mill. This dates from the late 18th century, though it may well have replaced an earlier mill. The grinding machinery, pit wheel and spur wheel are still in situ. During world war 2 bread was baked in ovens behind the mill. It can be visited, but only by appointment: ring Mr and Mrs Smith at 0909 730214. Pass in front of the mill to reach the church.

5: LANGOLD & HODSOCK PRIORY

Both Langold Country Park and Hodsock Priory are delightful places, and they are linked by unspoilt green lanes and field paths.

Distance: 8 miles

Time: 4 hours

Start: At the small car park near Langold Country Park, map reference SK 595866

Maps: Pathfinders SK 68/78 (East Retford) and SK 48/58 (Kiveton Park)

How to Get There:

By Car: Langold is 5 miles north of Worksop on the A60

By Bus: Services 20/21/22/24 hourly between Worksop and Doncaster

Refreshments: "Sherwood Ranger", "Blue Bell" and "Grey Horses", North Carlton

Nearest Tourist Information: Worksop Tourist Information Centre, Public Library, Memorial Avenue, Worksop (0909 501148)

Beside the small car park, grassy mounds protect the children's play area where once trains passed laden with coal from the nearby pit: Firbeck, which was open from 1926-68. Nearby, sidings are fast being colonised by birch and willow trees, supporting a variety of birds and butterflies.

Go around the mounds to the left and cross to the woodlands opposite. Soon after entering the wood turn left and follow a broad path. Maps show this as a dry lake, long since colonised by deciduous trees. The path emerges near Langold Lake, which was made in the early 19th century to complement a stately home, which was to stand on the

Langold Woods

northern bank. The foundations were laid in 1818, but it was never completed.

It is possible to walk along either side of the lake, where human swimmers coexist with coot and mallard. Bassetlaw District Council took over the running of the lake in 1974, the previous council having acquired it from the Coal Board. Like the former miners' cricket, bowling and football facilities, the lake was opened to the general public and provides swimming, fishing and children's play equipment for the whole district.

If following the right-hand bank, cross the bridge at the end and turn right to follow another, narrower lake popular with Canada geese. This lake gradually narrows to a stream, and soon you will find a stile on the left. The path is well defined across an arable field towards the former

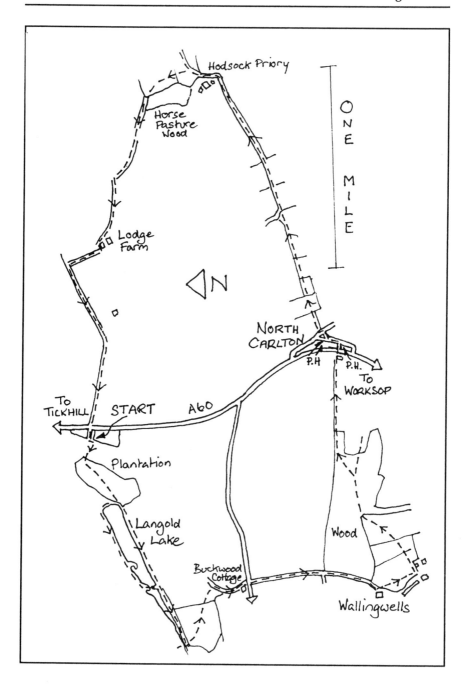

spoil-heap, now greened and planted with trees. Cross a stile and follow the farm-track to the right to Buckwood Cottage Farm.

Cross the road and continue along a lane. This bridleway passes through woodland to reach Wallingwells, formerly the site of a Benedictine nunnery, now a mansion in genteel decay. Beyond the handgate left the path runs parallel to the house's ornamental lake. Reaching a house, turn left to follow the well-trodden path across fields to Wallingwells Wood, where the main path follows a double row of ancient yews through mixed woodland. When the path forks, keep left to approach the edge of the wood where it borders a modern estate. A hedged path runs along the edge of the estate to join the A60 in Carlton-in-Lindrick.

This part of the village is North Carlton, a Conservation Area with a large number of houses built of locally quarried limestone. Across the road is the "Sherwood Ranger", with the "Blue Bell", a listed building, along to the left. Opposite the "Ranger", a fish and chip shop offers provender for hungry walkers. The route continues across the A60 (carefully) and down Chapel Lane. Keep left along Low Street past the "Grey Horses" and bear right to a T-junction. A few yards left along Greenway there is a narrow walled ginnel on the right, and the path continues through four meadows.

On joining a farm road turn right towards Hodsock Priory. At a T-junction, turn left past Priory Farm for a good view of the 16th-century gatehouse. The adjoining house was built to match the gatehouse: though it may look like a priory, it has never been one. Sir Andrew and Lady Buchanan open their gardens from time to time in aid of charity, and a visit is highly recommended, especially at cherry-blossom time.

Leave the drive to head for a farm gateway left and continue to another gate near the corner of Horsepasture Wood. Follow the lane for a mile to Hodsock Lodge Farm, skirt the stable yard and turn right along the drive. At the end, turn left to reach the A60, which you cross to return to your starting point.

6: HARWORTH & TICKHILL

This short walk links the Nottinghamshire mining village of Harworth with Tickhill in Yorkshire, a village steeped in history.

Distance: 4 miles

Time: 2 hours

Start: Common Lane, Harworth, map reference SK 611915

Maps: Pathfinder SK 49/59 (Rotherham) and SK 69/79 (Harworth & Gringley), Landranger 111 (Sheffield & Doncaster)

How to Get There:

By Car: Harworth is just off the A1, 3 miles north of Blyth

By Bus: Hourly services 21 and 25 daily from Doncaster, hourly services 29 and 30 between Retford & Bawtry. Sunday services sketchy

Refreshments: "Millstone" and "Carpenter's Arms", Tickhill, "Butcher's Arms", Harworth

Nearest Tourist Information: Doncaster Central Library, Waterdale, S. Yorkshire (0302 734309) or Worksop Tourist Information Centre, Public Library, Memorial Avenue, Worksop (0909 501148).

A mineshaft was sunk at the tiny village of Harworth by the Northern Union Mining Company in 1913. They used German capital, equipment and men, who arrived with immaculate timing to be interned during world war one. The next company to run the mine went bankrupt, and only in 1923 was a rich seam of coal found. It was Harworth coal which was burned by the Flying Scotsman when it did the London-Edinburgh run (392 miles) in 7 hours 27 minutes.

Park in Common Lane, Harworth, taking care not to cause any obstruction. Follow this lane until it becomes a hedged farm road: after a

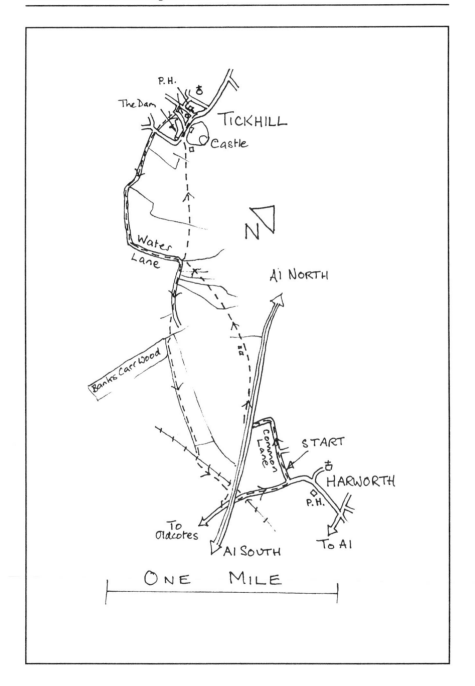

hundred yards take the lane on the left, which passes underneath the A1,, then runs beside it briefly before resuming its original line. After passing a lone house the route continues as a well-marked field path. After the first field only a wooden finger-post marks the county boundary with South Yorkshire, and the clear path continues to a substantial wooden bridge. Beyond the bridge there are two paths, both of which lead to Tickhill: the most direct route is to the left across three more fields. There is now another bridge to the left, but our route is across two meadows to Tickhill.

The visitor to Tickhill, crossing the old brick bridge and passing through a farmyard, is greeted by the strange sight of ducks swimming past at eye level. Across a leafy lane is the Dam, an old mill-pond whose mill,

The dam, Tickhill

recently renovated as a dwelling, is just to the left. Turn right between the Dam and the deep moat of Tickhill Castle.

The Norman castle, which is privately owned, was built soon after the Norman conquest by Roger de Busli, William the Conqueror's son-in-law. It was fortified by the Earl of Shrewsbury in 1102 against the king, Henry I. This move was counter-productive, as the earl was banished and Henry became the new owner.

During the 12th century the curtain wall and gatehouse were built and the keep strengthened. The civil war found the Royalists holding the castle against Parliament, but they were obliged to surrender in 1644. Soon afterwards the castle was "slighted" so that it could no longer be defended, and the stone of the keep was removed by the Hansby family to build a large house which still stands in the grounds.

Continue along Castlegate, with a good view of the gatehouse, built about 1100. It is over 10 metres high and 2 metres thick. There are traces of an upper room above the portcullis. At the next corner is the Millstone, a large pub and restaurant, while the smaller family-owned Carpenters Arms is opposite. At this point a small detour is possible straight ahead on Castlegate to the centre of Tickhill, with its shops, church, old buildings and impressive Butter Cross. An informative leaflet about the town can be picked up at the library as you pass.

The main walk turns left at the Millstone, then left again along Dam Road. This soon becomes a fenced footpath, to be followed past the Town Council's Wild Flower Meadow, then across a road to enter Water Lane.

The lane twists and turns for a mile, accompanied by a tiny stream, ending at a stile. Cross the grass field and an impressive footbridge, then follow a track winding right past a wood and along the hedge to a railway crossing. Cross the single line with due care and follow the track to the Styrrup road. A pavement has thoughtfully been provided to take you back, after a left turn, to Harworth.

7: SUTTON & LOUND

*The walk links the twin villages of Sutton and Lound in the plain by the river
Idle. The area has been worked for sand and gravel since 1879, resulting in
quite a few lakes used for recreation or habitat for wild life.*

Distance: 9 miles

Time: 4.5 hours

Start: Sutton church, map reference SK 681849

Maps: Pathfinder SK 68/78 (East Retford North), Landranger 120 (Mansfield & Worksop)

How to Get There:

By Car: Just off the A634, 3 miles north of Retford

By Bus: Retford to Bawtry services 27, 27A and 27B, which are rare on
Sundays

Nearest Tourist Information: Retford Tourist Information Centre,
Amcott House, 40 Grove Street, Retford (0777 860780)

Start at Sutton church, at the north end of the village. Go through the
kissing gate to the right and follow the track past the churchyard. Cross
a stile left and follow the wide track at the edge of the first field: like
many lanes and tracks in this area there is a wealth of wild flowers.
Continue beside a second field, across an earth bridge and round the
corner of the third, now following the main East Coast railway.

Reaching a track, turn left into an area recently planted with oak and ash
trees. Round the corner, there is an obvious track ahead, but angle left to
follow the faint public footpath which passes through the young trees
and runs close to the railway. This can be overgrown at first as it skirts
pools lined with reed mace, but becomes a wide grass track along the
edge of the Daneshill Lakes reserve.

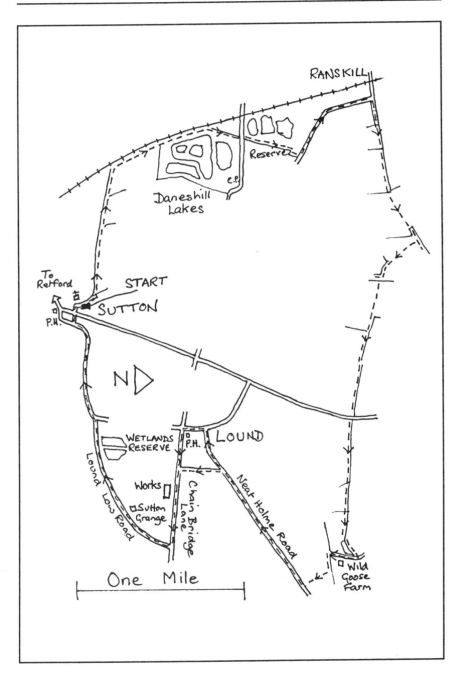

Daneshill Lakes Local Nature Reserve covers 50 hectares straddling the Torworth-Lound road. The gravel workings were vacated by the Steetley company in 1968 and regenerated naturally. Nottinghamshire County Council bought the land in 1982 and developed it for a variety of uses. The first stretch of water encountered is South Lake, which is used for sailing, angling and windsurfing while still attracting a variety of bird life, while part of the land is set aside as a Schools Nature Reserve.

The old pits beyond Daneshill Road are managed by Nottinghamshire Wildlife Trust to provide habitat for as many wild creatures as possible.

Opposite the main track to the lake an enormous sign informs railway travellers that they are 250 miles from Edinburgh. Finally a notice reading "Daneshill Piggery. Private Property. Keep Out" leads you to suspect that the adjacent kissing-gate might be the correct route. Pass the very unfriendly dogs and cross Daneshill Road to the Nature Reserve. Pass straight along the edge of the reserve, keeping right at the far end along a narrow path to a wide hedged lane.

Turn left here to pass a couple of firms specialising in tyres, scrap and paving slabs and reach a T-junction beside a woodyard. Turn right in another lane, negotiate a gate, then follow the track to an enormous stile. As you walk at the edge of a grass field, you may see swans which nest in an old gravel-pit on your right, while hordes of rabbits scutter away to their sandy burrows. Cross two stiles and a tiny stream, continue across grassland and through a gateway heading for Hill Farm (15 metres above sea level!). After 100 yards, turn right beside a solitary silver birch. After a quarter of a mile this track turns sharp right: after the corner turn left, follow the clear path across an arable field and continue beside an old gravel-pit and the scattered traces of Ellis Plantation. Join its access track which takes you to a road.

Cross the road, go carefully down the grass bank and along the edge of the right-hand field. After this large field continue beside an even bigger one, through a hedge and on to a strip of woodland. Here the path swings left beside the wood to a farm track. Turn right to pass Wild Goose Farm and carry straight on with a tall hawthorn hedge on your left. Moves are afoot to divert this path to the left, in which case it will be clearly waymarked. It will still bring you to Neat Holme Road, a hedged lane.

At this point you turn right and follow the lane for half a mile, then pass through a slip stile on the left just before the lane narrows as it enters Lound. A pleasant path, dedicated by Tarmac, runs alongside yet another old gravel pit. A row of poplars guards one side of the path, while a wide variety of native species have been planted between path and waterside. At the end, turn left along Chain Bridge Lane.

Alternatively you could continue in Neatholme Road into the village of Lound, turning left to reach the Blue Bell and a drink (no food provided). The village of Lound is a settlement on slightly higher ground beside the Idle valley, and the main street – Town Street – which you have followed was a track along the scarp. The older buildings with gables facing the street indicate the old Tofts, narrow strips of land running back from the road.

Turn left just past the pub into Chain Bridge Lane. Pass the enormous Tarmac works and a quarter of a mile beyond, nearly opposite a water sports centre, take the Lound Low Road on your right. This lane leads past the attractive Sutton Grange and Low Farm to the fascinating Wetlands Waterfowl Reserve, which offers 32 acres of great interest to bird-watchers: two lakes stocked with water birds from all over the world, woodland walks and a "children's' farmyard". It also has a cafe available to parched walkers.

Not far past the Reserve you join a road flanked by a tarmac footpath, which you follow straight ahead to Sutton. On entering the village turn right along Church Way to return to the start.

8: MATTERSEY & EVERTON

Until recent times, the delightful Nottinghamshire village of Everton was separated from the Isle of Axholme in Lincolnshire by swampy ground, where the river Idle flowed sluggishly towards the Trent. Now the land has been drained and good farmland lies beneath the Barrow Hills. This easy walk from the historic village of Mattersey offers varied views and pleasant surprises.

Distance: 6 or 8 miles

Time: 3 or 4 hours

Start: Mattersey church, map reference SK 691894

Maps: Pathfinders SK 68/78 (East Retford) and SK 69/79 (Harworth & Gringley), Landranger 111 (Sheffield & Doncaster)

How to Get There:

By Car: Mattersey is 4 miles south-east of Bawtry on the A631

By Bus: Services 27, 27A, 27B, 28 2-hourly between Retford and Bawtry, 83 twice daily linking Gaisborough, Worksop and Retford

Refreshments: Barley Mow, Mattersey and Blacksmith's Arms, Everton

---

Start at Mattersey church and go down the lane between it and the "Barley Mow" to cross the river Idle. This pleasant lane, recently pedestrianised, brings you to a by-road where turn right. After passing Rye Hall Farm, turn left through a forest of Scots pine on a sandy path. Pass Pusto Hill Farm, which was built in the 18th century by squire Jonathan Acklom, a prodigious improver of his estate at nearby Wiseton. The "model farm" is still a striking sight from the east. Follow the lane ahead, with a view of the four-storey ruined mill to the left. A mill on this site was first mentioned in 1344, but the mill we see was built in 1830. Towards the end of the century it was converted to steam power: the chimney still stands though it has had no function for 60 years. At the A631, which follows the line of a Roman road, cross carefully to the

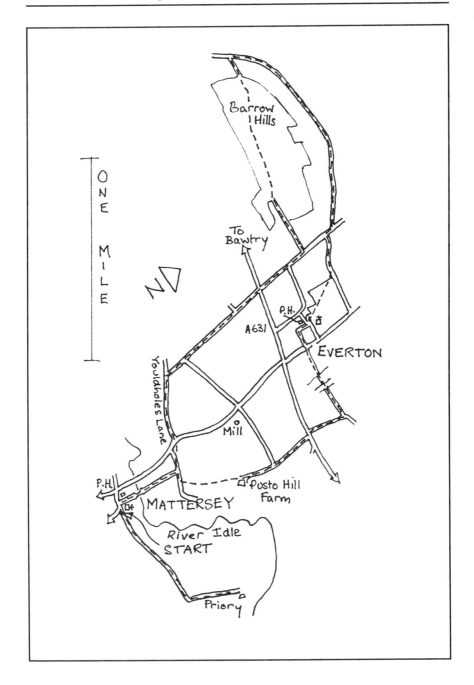

farm lane leading to Park Farm.

Where the lane swings right, take the track on the left, passing a barn and crossing a small arable field to a stile. Follow the hedge ahead, cross the stile near the corner of a garden, and continue along the snicket into Everton village. Cross the road to Brewery Lane and at the end, with the site of the eponymous brewery on your right, turn right along Post Office Street.

On your left is the charming 17th century house named "Wisteria Cottage". In summer the reason for this name is gloriously obvious. This street leads to the diminutive green with its oak tree commemorating Edward VII's coronation. The "Blacksmith's" is on your left, the stately Norman church on the right.

On Trinity Sundays, a ceremony takes place here when, half-way through singing the hymn "We Love the Place oh God", the congregation go outside and join hands to encircle the church. After a prayer they return to complete the hymn. This is known as "clipping the church". If you visit the church, admire the curious creatures over the door. Are they salamanders or dragons?

Pass left of the church along a narrowing lane, then on entering a field go half-left to the end of a hedge and diagonally across the open field. Pass through the hedge, then drop down into the narrow Middle Cross Lane. Turn left, then right at the end. Pass Rock Cottage and bear left, noting the attractive terra-cotta panels on "Lark Rise" opposite. Follow Pasture Lane for a mile, till you find a lone ash tree guarding the path into Barrow Hills Wood.

It seems likely that these hills would have provided an easily defensible site for settlement in pre-Roman times, but no evidence has been found to confirm this. In the wood take the right fork which takes you up the hill and straight through this delightful woodland. Leave the wood by a kissing-gate and go down Pinfold Lane.

At Harwell Lane, turn right through the tiny hamlet of Harwell to the A631. Cross this again and continue along a sandy lane, finally dropping down through a hollow-way to a T-junction. Here you turn left along Youldholes Lane and at a road cross half-right to cut off the corner. Very shortly you can turn right to follow your outward route into Mattersey. Unlike many country pubs which are closed to thirsty ramblers in the afternoon, the "Barley Mow" rarely shuts its doors.

Barrow Hills from the south

It would be a pity to miss a visit to the ruined Mattersey Priory. To reach it, pass the church and follow Abbey Road for about a mile, returning by the same route. The abbey lies in a lovely site near the river. It was a priory of the Order of Saint Gilbert of Sempringham, the only entirely English monastic order. When founded, it had six regular canons, who were ordained priests, with ten lay brethren to work in the priory fields. Only a few fragments remain of this Gilbertine foundation which was first built about 1185, for much of the stone went to build the Manor House.

In Mattersey church can be seen two 14th century panels from the abbey. They show Saint Martin sharing his cloak with a beggar and Saint Helena allegedly finding "the true cross".

Mattersey Priory and Farm

9: DRAKEHOLES, CLAYWORTH & GRINGLEY ON THE HILL

Most of the walk follows a loop in the Chesterfield canal, linked by field paths and lanes. It offers the opportunity to visit three small but delightful villages.

Distance: 8.5 miles

Time: 4 hours

Start: Park in the lay-by near the canal at Drakeholes, opposite the Griff Inn, map reference SK 707903

Maps: Pathfinders SK 69/79 (Harworth) and SK 68/78 (East Retford), Landranger 112 (Scunthorpe) and 120 (Mansfield and Worksop)

How to Get There:

By Car: By the A631 between Tickhill and Gainsborough

By Bus: Service 96 between Retford and Gainsborough, hourly Monday to Saturday

Refreshments: "Brewers Arms", Clayworth, "Blue Bell", Gringley and "Griff Inn", Drakeholes

Nearest Tourist Information: Retford Tourist Information Centre, Amcott House, 40, Grove Street, Retford (0777 860780)

Join the canal and follow the tow-path to the right. Pass under Lady Bridge, also known as Old Man Bridge because of the bearded heads on both parapets. At Taylor's Bridge (number 71) it is possible to detour through the delightful village of Wiseton to the right. We have to thank squire Jonathan Acklom who in the 18th century not only improved the village but built some spectacular local farms and the "White Swan", now called the Griff Inn, at Drakeholes.

The Griff Inn and Drakeholes Tunnel

Leaving the canal we pass the gentrified work-yard and then a cottage on the right whose chimneys reveal its origin as the estate laundry. Turn left opposite two decorative cottages and pass the 18th century Grange Farm to reach Wiseton Top Bridge. Turn right again, and after a short stretch of road continue along the towpath past Gray's Bridge to Otter Bridge.

On your left it is hard to miss Royston Manor House, originally built in 1588 as the home of the Otter family. After a chequered history it was totally renovated in 1891, when most of the mullioned windows were refurbished. During the War it was a home for evacuated children, and then became an hotel. At the time of writing it is for sale. Cross Otter Bridge and turn immediately right along the signposted path. Pass the massive coach-house and pigeon-cote of the 18th century Grange Farm and head half-left to a stile by the gate in the corner of the meadow. Pass Beck Lane Farm to the road.

The Brewers' Arms is 100 yards left, our route is across the road to the lane opposite, then right into Mill Lane. You are now following the Trent

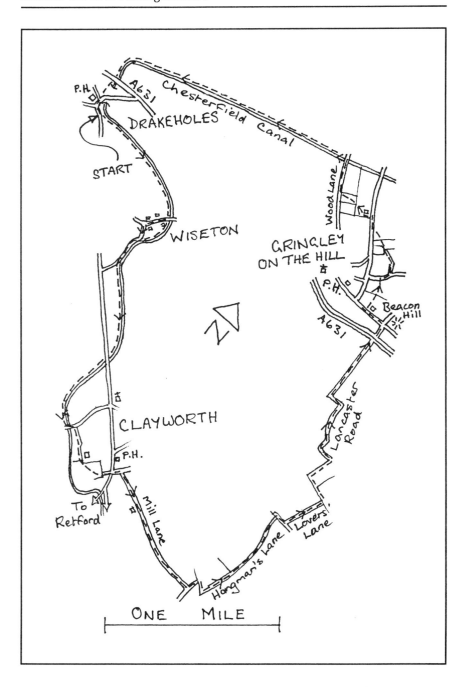

Valley Way, past the Mill House where no evidence is seen of the post mill which stood there. After three quarters of a mile you should see the wavy blue arrow of the Way pointing left along Hangman's Lane. At the top of the hill, in a wide grassy area, turn right then left into Lovers' Lane, overgrown but with a path cleared by Nottinghamshire County Council. Cross a footbridge at the end, turn left along the edge of two fields then right to reach a lane. Follow it to the A631 road, with good views of Gringley-on-the-Hill.

This attractive village is said to be a healthy place to live, high and dry in winter and bracing in summer. It can be very bracing in the winter when the north wind blows across the Carrs. Cross the road with care and go up to the crossroads. There is public access to Beacon Hill on the right, the site of a prehistoric fortress. It offers wide views across former fenlands to the Isle of Axholme on the horizon. It is said that Lincoln Cathedral and Beverley, Selby and York Minsters can be seen from here, but I can only vouch for the first.

Our route lies to the left and through a kissing-gate right just past the manor house. Here you could detour straight ahead to the Blue Bell for refreshment, and perhaps visit the heart of the old village, its cross and Norman church.

Go down the meadow to a stile and continue to a stone stile. Turn right as far as Pitt Lane on the left and at the end cross two stiles into a meadow. Follow the row of hawthorns to another stile, then go through a gate to reach the road beside a double signpost. Turn right down the road for a few yards, then left past a barn. Cross the stile and angle left across two fields to Wood Lane.

Follow the lane down to Gringley Top Lock and turn left to follow the towpath for two miles. This is a most attractive wooded section with coots and moorhens in residence and perhaps a kingfisher and a few bats. When the canal swings sharp left to Drakeholes tunnel, go up the slope and head for the distinctive shape of the Griff Inn.

10: MISTERTON & WEST STOCKWITH

In a walk that patrols the north-eastern borders of the County there is a contrast in watercourses as we follow the banks of the Idle, the Trent and the Chesterfield Canal.

Distance: 4.5 miles

Time: 2 hours

Start: Misterton church, map reference SK 965947

Maps: Pathfinder SK 69/79 (Harworth), Landranger 112 (Scunthorpe)

How to Get There:

By Car: Misterton is on the A161 between Beckingham, where it joins the A631, and Haxey on the Isle of Axholme

By Bus: Frequent services 95, 96, 97 and 98 (Retford/Gainsborough), 83 (twice a day) Gainsborough-Worksop

Refreshments: "White Hart", "Waterside Inn" and "Miniature World", West Stockwith, "Packet Inn" and "Red Lion", Misterton

Nearest Tourist Information: Retford Tourist Information Centre, Amcott House, 40 Grove Street, Retford (0777 860780)

Start at Misterton church, cross the road and set off along Haxey Road, passing the Old Vicarage, a 16th century timber-framed house. Turn right into a hedged path signposted "Misterton Soss and West Stockwith": the sign is high up and can be obscured by trees. On reaching a grass field turn left to a stile in the corner, then right in what until recently was a ridge and furrow meadow, but is now arable. At the end of the field the path crosses a stile and heads diagonally right to the corner of the field, where the hedge ends: however it is clearly local practice to turn right and then left along the field headland. Continue straight across the next field, cross the dyke by the bridge and turn right to go round the corner of an arable field.

West Stockwith Lock

The route is now a straight line beside a hedge, with a couple of plank bridges on the way, then cross-field, then alongside a drainage ditch. This may be overgrown in summer, so watch your step. Fine wooden stairs take you up a railway embankment. You cross the line angling half-right and wondering why British Rail provide excellent steps on either side of the line and leave you to negotiate the line and the granite ballast with no secure surface to walk on. The path passes a pleasant lake, then goes between fields to Soss Lane. As you turn left you have a good view of the old pumping station, built in 1828 but now superseded and left to crumble away.

Just past the pumping station is the River Idle. It was here that a soss, or sluice, was built by the Dutchman, Cornelius Vermuyden, to drain the Carrs, the swampy land in the Idle valley. A lock was later needed for

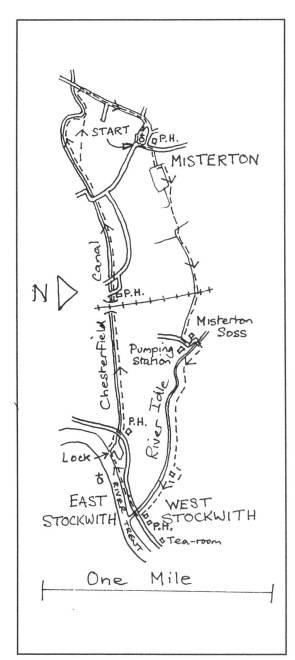

boat traffic up the river to Bawtry. there was more drainage work in the late 18th century when a triple sluice was built here, and the Mother Drain was cut from the Soss 10 miles up river. The pumping station was the first steam engine used for land drainage outside the Fens.

Cross the bridge just to the left, turn right and follow the river, leaving it only to go round the new pumping station. Return to the floodbank for a short distance, then follow a fenced path and pass under the archway of a house marked 1785 to reach the main street of West Stockwith. This quiet village, facing East Stockwith across the Trent in Lincolnshire, was once a hive of industry, with 4 boatyards, 5 roperies, a flax works and a chemical works.

On the left you will find the White Hart, and a few yards beyond, a shop and tearoom with a tiny but attractive garden. This is also "Miniature World", a museum of dolls and doll's houses.

Our route, however, is to the right, after noting the notice-board opposite proclaiming the end of the Trent Valley Way (or perhaps the beginning, depending on your viewpoint). This linear route follows the Trent valley for 84 miles, and was inaugurated to celebrate the 100th anniversary of the County Council. Soon a signpost diverts you onto the floodbank to pass West Stockwith basin and its marina, always packed with vessels of all sizes.

A narrow bridge crosses the lock which gives access from the Trent to the Chesterfield Canal, but only when the tide is high, for the river is tidal as far as Cromwell Lock, a few miles from Newark. This was the trans-shipment point from river to canal or vice versa, and here was the boatyard which made the unique Chesterfield canal boats known as "Cuckoos". These horse-drawn craft were 70 feet long and 6 feet 10 inches wide, carrying cargoes up to 24 tons. They took 2 days to do the 26 miles to Worksop. It is now a centre for pleasure boating.

Swing right around the basin and climb up to the road. Crossing the canal bridge, the Waterside Inn is ahead: on the left, immediately before the pub, is the tow-path which brings us back to Misterton. A row of tall willows shade the route to the Packet Inn, whose copious menu includes 32-ounce steaks. The pub's unusual name, which it shares with another near Gas House Bridge in Retford, commemorates the passenger boats which ran on market days to Retford from outlying villages. Just beyond are Misterton Low Lock and Top Lock and a couple of bridges, then the tow-path backs on to village gardens.

After passing under Wharf Bridge (number 81) the tow-path circles round the village. Across the water, Jersey cows make a pleasant change from the black and white Freisians which have taken over in recent years. On the right, the field lies fallow pending discussions about a proposed new Marina, with chandlery, restaurant and heaven knows what else. Meanwhile, there is a footpath which cuts off the loop in the canal.

Just before the next bridge, Coopers bridge, turn right to join the road and walk into Misterton, turning right along Church Street and passing

through the churchyard. The rather startling buildings on the right are a village hall and vicarage. The church, an unpretentious one with a stubby broach spire, is worth a visit. John Piper's unusual east window of the Tree of Life is a recent addition, but I liked the 14th-century head at the end of the arcade, whose huge ears are traditionally embellished with tomatoes at harvest festival time.

11: BECKINGHAM & SAUNDBY

A Trent Valley walk to the isolated farmstead of Clayworth Woodhouse, on a plateau between the rivers Trent and Idle.

Distance: 5 miles

Time: 2.5 hours

Start: Beckingham Church, map reference SK 779903

Map: Pathfinder

How to Get There:

By Car: Take the A620 from Retford.

By Bus: Regular service between Retford and Gainsborough (95, 95A, 96, 97, 98) Monday to Saturday, sketchy on Sunday. A couple of buses daily from Worksop (83).

Refreshments: "Crown" and cafe, Saundby, "Hare and Hounds", Beckingham.

Start at the mediaeval Beckingham church. Enter Rectory Road which runs past the west end of the church, signed "Private Road", and almost immediately go along the snicket to the right. Go through an elaborate iron gate at the end, turn left for 40 yards, then right into Ravenscroft Road and follow it to the A631.

Cross the road to a footbridge and stile and follow the path along the edge of the field and straight on to join the corner of a lane. Go straight ahead to South Sandy Furze Farm, through the yard and ahead again. This long path meets another in mid-field: turn left here to join Wood Lane, which you are to follow for a mile, passing through Beckingham Wood.

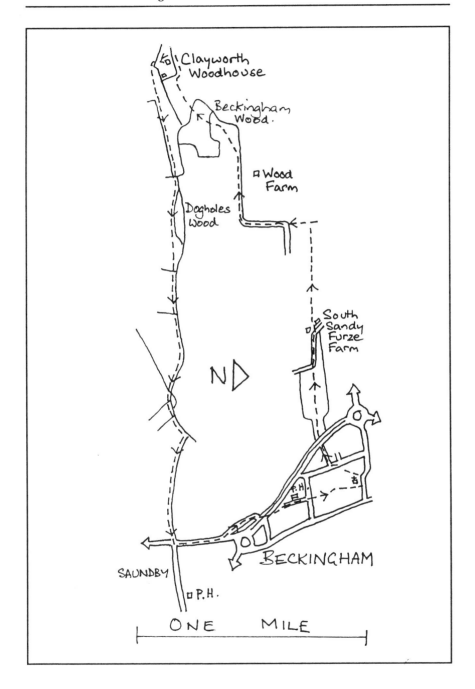

On reaching the gateway to Clayworth Woodhouse you have to leave the lane, turn right and walk around three sides of the complex of house, barns and outbuildings. Finally cross a paddock to join the farm track as it enters the field, where you turn left. Pass to the south of the house alongside a thicket marking the edge of a pond. Follow the same line cross-field to the end of a field boundary and follow it to the end of the field. Here cross the bridge on your right and immediately turn left.

Follow the edge of Dogholes Wood and at the end keep ahead to a footbridge. Follow the field boundary to a stile and continue along the foot of a grass field. After a step-stile beside a horse-jump, skirt the edge of a little wood for about 40 yards and cross another step-stile. The area in front of you has been recently planted with a variety of deciduous trees, some of which are losing the battle with thistles and giant hogweed. Keep to the edge of this area, cross a bridge and go along the edge of the next field, then turn right along the top to reach Bar Road.

Opposite, the thirsty can find relief at Rosie's Truck Stop and Cafe, or 200 yards ahead along Ramper Road, the "Crown". To the left is Beckingham: walk along Bar Road South to the left of the roundabout, cross the by-pass and turn left to enter Bar Road North on the right, which joins at an angle.

Croft Farm, on your right, is a listed building dating from 1660, and an impressive house from the same period is just before the "Hare and Hounds". The "oversized" gables are a clue that the house was once thatched. Pass the Hare and Hounds unless you need a snack or a glass of something, go straight ahead at the crossroads to another iron gate and follow the pleasant village footpath back to the church.

12: HAYTON CASTLE & CLAYWORTH

There are views over the valleys of the Idle and the Trent on this easy-to-follow walk, which also follows a Farm Trail and part of the Chesterfield Canal.

Distance: 8 miles

Time: 4 hours

Start: Hayton Castle Farm Trail car park, map reference SK 740867

Maps: Pathfinder SK 68/78 (East Retford), Landranger 120 (Mansfield & the Dukeries)

How to Get There:

By Car: Hayton Castle Farm is off Tilbridge Lane, the road between Clayworth and North Wheatley

By Bus: 95/96/97 and 98 between Retford and Gainsborough hourly

Refreshments: "Brewer's Arms", Clayworth, "Boat Inn", Hayton

Nearest Tourist Information: Retford Tourist Information Centre, Amcott House, 40, Grove Street, Retford (0777 860780)

The walk starts at the site of a twelfth century moated farmstead which is also the car park for a Farm Trail. It was Marjorie and Len Campion who in 1985 created the trail at Hayton Castle Farm, winning awards for conservation and for the trail itself. The trail is open to the public every day except Christmas Day.

The first part of our walk follows the trail, first heading across the ancient site towards the Chesterfield Canal. Designed by James Brindley, the canal was opened in 1777 to link Chesterfield with the river Trent. Now only pleasure boats ply between the Trent and Worksop. Like

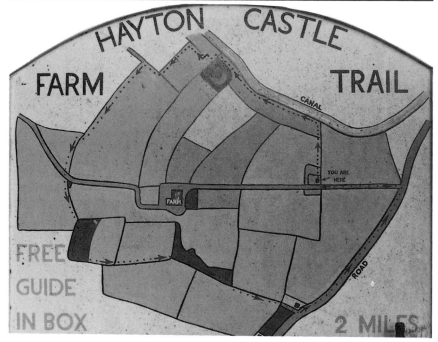

Hayton Castle Farm

many residents of Hayton, those at Hayton Castle Farm once used the canal for their water supply, and until 1945 water was pumped up to the house. The four-inch cast-iron pipe they used can still be seen.

Turn left along the canal-side meadow which shows the ridges and furrows of mediaeval cultivation but is now permanent grazing. Next we meet "The Old Brickyard", a small wood which Retford Young Farmers have turned into a habitat for water birds. There is a small display of clay products from Hayton Castle brickyard. Turn left at the end of the wood, then right beside a field where Roman remains have been found. Follow the clear track round the edges, past the end of a grassy lane and an old fox covert. When you join the wide grass bridleway, the trail is following a public right of way which was once the route of the road from Hayton to Clayworth.

At this point, the walker would be well rewarded by a small detour to the right as far as the top of the hill. To the left there is a view across the

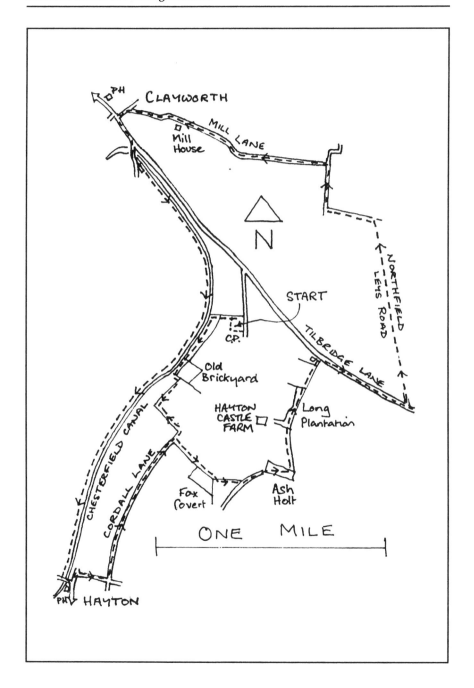

Trent Valley and, on a clear day, a glimpse of Lincoln Cathedral. To the right is the Idle valley and its quarry lagoons, with the Derbyshire hills in the distance.

Retrace your steps to the bottom of the hill and keep right on the footpath to Ash Holt, a small, ancient wood replanted in the 1980s to repair the ravages of Dutch Elm disease. In the 18th century, when Castle Farm was new, this was the only wood in the parish. There is a "hide" used by the Young Ornithologists' Club and a resident fox. Follow the winding path through the wood, then along field edges to Long Plantation, where more replanting is seen of oak, ash, horse chestnut, wild cherry, hazel and guelder rose.

After a rest on the seats provided, with a fine view along the canal towards Clayworth, continue to the road. This is Tilbridge Lane, once a Roman road from Doncaster *(Danum)* to Lincoln *(Lindum)* which crossed the river Trent at Littleborough. Turning right up a sharp rise, you will soon see the Trent valley. It would be hard to miss the power stations at West Burton, slightly left, and Cottam further up the valley, bringing employment to the area and acid rain to Europe.

Drop down towards North Wheatley, but turn left into Northfield Leys Road, a farm track climbing steadily north. Turn left at a gap in the hedge ahead: a wavy blue waymark indicates the Trent Valley Way, a County Council route following the Trent valley across Nottinghamshire. Turn right when the hedge ends. Ahead is the intriguing Hangman's Lane, but our route is to the left along a hedged green lane, Mill Lane. This passes the Mill House, then soon afterwards dives left to Clayworth main street. To the right the "Brewer's Arms" offers refreshment, but the route is left to the hump-backed Clayworth Bridge over the canal. After crossing, join the canal beside the Retford & Worksop Boat Club, which until 1969 was the "White Hart" pub. The two-mile stretch of the canal between here and Hayton is a peaceful one with no bridges, so is popular with ducks, swans, moorhens, herons and other species. Halfway along, you will recognise the Farm Trail on the opposite bank.

Leaving the canal at the "Boat Inn", cross the bridge, turn left and then right up the hill. The first lane on the left is Cordall Lane, which brings you back to the Farm Trail. Turning left, follow it in reverse order to your starting point.

Chesterfield Canal at Clayworth

13: BOLE

This short walk follows both the present and former banks of the Trent. A well-maintained grass path, following the old course of the river, offers a wealth of flowers each Spring. After a towpath stroll, return across fields to the village.

Distance: 4 miles

Time: 2 hours

Start: Bole church, map reference SK 793871

Maps: Pathfinder SK 68/78 (East Retford North) and 88/98 (Gainsborough South), Landranger 121 (Lincoln)

How to Get There:

By Car: Bole is at the end of a narrow lane off the A620 Retford –Gainsborough road.

By Bus: Two-hourly service 95 and 95B between Retford and Gainsborough

Refreshments: None

Nearest Tourist Information: Retford Tourist Information Centre, Amcott House, 40 Grove Street, Retford (0777 860780)

Start at Bole church. Walk down the hill past Manor Farm, a listed building dating from 1675. Its distinctive gables show the Dutch influence which came to this area with Vermuyden. Cross the railway by the level crossing, go straight on between enormous hedges, then after fifty yards turn left. There are the rusting remains of a kissing-gate, then a metal footbridge. A narrow grass path leads between rampant hawthorn on one side and uncultivated land, producing healthy thistles and willow herb, on the other.

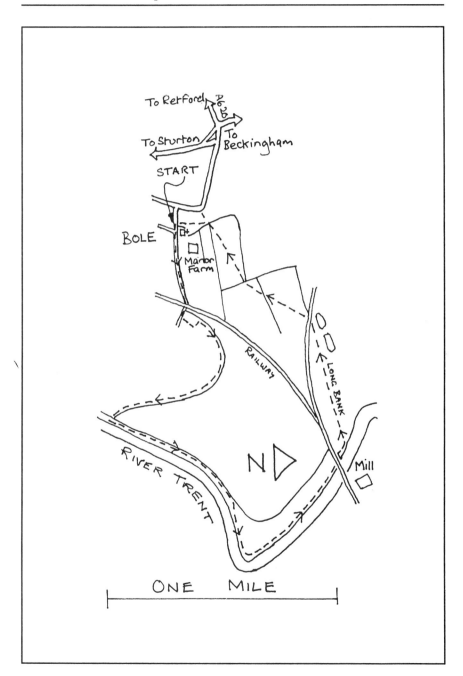

Presently the path swings sharp left at another rusty gate, then crosses a plank bridge. A wide, grass path crosses a wide, flat valley and swings right alongside a high hedge of ancient hawthorn colonised by elder bushes. The marshy valley on your right harbours meadowsweet and cranesbill. This is an old course of the Trent, a river whose meanders in its shallow valley have left many "ox-bows" like this one. This part of the Trent's course was by-passed in 1792 following heavy floods.

Finally the path climbs to the Trent flood-bank. After climbing a fence, turn left to follow the river downstream towards Gainsborough on the far bank. The featureless bulk of Spillers mill is already only too obvious. Keep on the floodbank until the riverside meadow opens up: here the path drops down to the river bank, goes round a sharp bend and passes a sign saying "86km". After passing under the railway bridge angle left on a farm track but then keep right to cross Saundby Beck by the stiles provided.

Start the return lap by turning left to walk along the floodbank beside the beck. Don't be tempted to drop down beside the fishing lakes, but continue along the floodbank to a stile beside the railway. Cross the lines at an angle, following the same line as before, then descend the embankment to another stile.

Head 45 degrees right across the grass field to a wooden bridge to the left of the corner of the field, then keep the same line to a stile into the adjacent field. Angle across the field to the far corner, entering a paddock where uneven ground marks the site of ancient fish-ponds. Turn left and pass right of the church to a gate.

14: STURTON-LE-STEEPLE & LITTLEBOROUGH

There is little obvious evidence in the tiny village of Littleborough that Roman legions crossed the Trent there on their way from Lincoln to Doncaster, from the massive garrison town of Lindum Colonia to the staging post at Danum en route for the northern frontier. An easy walk makes use of the network of green lanes in the Trent valley and follows an attractive stretch of the river itself.

Distance: 7 miles

Time: 3.5 hours

Start: Sturton-le-Steeple church, map reference SK 788838

Maps: Pathfinders SK 68/78 (East Retford North) and SK 88/98 (Gainsborough South), Landranger 121 (Lincoln)

How to Get There:

By Car: Sturton is 5 miles east of Retford via the A620 and Tilbridge Lane

By Bus: Service 95 between Retford and Gainsborough every couple of hours

Refreshments: "The Reindeer", Sturton-le-Steeple

Nearest Tourist Information: Retford Tourist Information Centre, Amcott House, 40 Grove Street, Retford (0777 860780)

Start near Sturton-le-Steeple church. The church was a twelfth-century foundation dedicated to Saint Peter and Saint Paul, set in a delightful wooded churchyard. Despite the image conjured up by the name of the village, it has never had a spire, though it does have twelve pinnacles around its tower instead of the eight typical of Nottinghamshire churches.

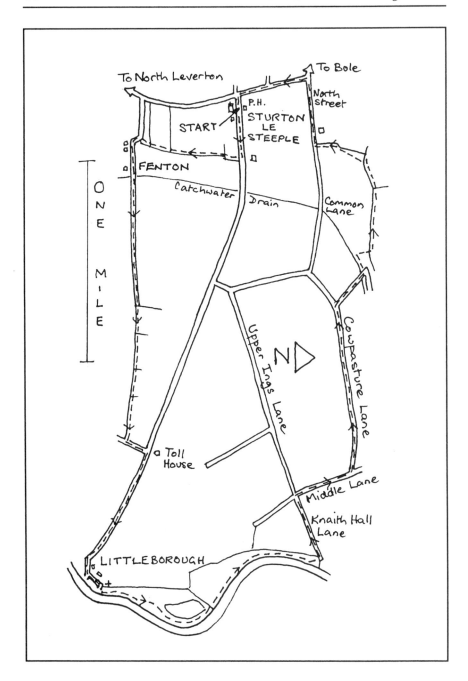

Walk east along the Littleborough road, leaving the village and turning right as signposted through a gate opposite the 17th century Manor Farm. Walk across a grass field, then along the edge of three more fields, watching out for rabbit-holes. On joining Three Leys Lane turn left past the tiny hamlet of Fenton. Both Grange Farm and Manor Farm date back to the 17th century, the latter having a coat of arms on its outbuilding. Fenton Grange has the initials W.M. and the date 1693 on its facade. The road through Fenton becomes a track: at a gate, go on along field edges to Thornhill Lane.

A short distance left is the hexagonal Littleborough Cottage, once a toll-house when the road was busier. At the toll-house, turn right to Littleborough and the river Trent. Here the Romans crossed the Trent by a stone-paved ford and called the village Segelocum. Their successors for many centuries forded the Trent here – including King Harold hurrying from one battle with the Vikings to another against William of Normandy – but in 1820 the Trent Navigation Company removed the 18-foot wide ford. A ferry undertook the crossing, a bridge was proposed, but the decision was taken to build one at Dunham, and Littleborough became a quiet and charming backwater.

Toll-house

Before continuing the walk downstream, a visit to the tiny church would be rewarding. The walls of the ancient Norman building are a patchwork, with herring-bone masonry and even some Roman tiles salvaged from the abandoned homes of earlier invaders. It has now been declared redundant and awaits its fate.

Follow the river bank to the left, at first on the flood bank, then pass right of a lake much favoured by swans. Pass a clapper-gate opposite the aptly-named Red Hill, then continue almost to the next gate. At this point you see Knaith Hall on the other bank, in Lincolnshire. This was a priory for Cistercian nuns.

Drop down to a stile left to join Knaith Hall Lane, one of a number of green lanes criss-crossing this land saved from the vagaries of the river by floodbanks. Take Middle Lane on the right which follows the Mother Drain. On reaching a bridge on the left across this, turn left along Cowpasture Lane. This could take you back to Sturton, but soon after passing a small wood on the left, there is an enjoyable detour. Take the lane on the right which crosses the Catchwater Drain.

After crossing the bridge another detour is possible, this time to the right and by a roundabout route to the deserted village of West Burton. The tiny village, which gave its name to the power station, had 15 houses in 1750. By 1865 only the church and a ruined farmhouse remained, and soon afterwards the church too was demolished. The churchyard, however, remains and rabbits tunnelling through it throw up skulls and bones.

Turn left to follow the edge of the romantically named Catchwater Drain for about 200 yards, then turn right to a stile and signpost in the hedge opposite. Turn left after the stile, keep along the hedge, then turn right at the end to a substantial footbridge. Cross the footbridge and turn left beside a row of coppiced ash. This pleasant path follows the wooded banks of a narrow stream as far as a plank bridge and stile. Continue in a grass field.

On reaching an earth bridge left, cross it and the high fences which protect it, then head across the meadow, converging with the right-hand hedge where it bends. Follow the hedge to Common Lane, go right to a junction, then left through the village to the pub and church.

15: STURTON-LE-STEEPLE & NORTH LEVERTON

An easy to follow walk on green lanes and field paths. There are fine views from the ridge above the Trent plain, and a splendid windmill to visit.

Distance: 7 miles

Time: 3.5 miles

Start: Sturton-le-Steeple church, map reference SK 788838

Maps: Pathfinder SK 68/78 (East Retford North), Landranger 120 (Mansfield & Worksop)

How to Get There:

By Car: Sturton is 5 miles east of Retford via the A620 and Tilbridge Lane

By Bus: Two-hourly services 95 and 95A between Retford and Gainsborough

Refreshments: "Royal Oak", North Leverton, "Reindeer Inn", Sturton

Nearest Tourist Information: Retford Tourist Information Centre, Amcott House, 40 Grove Street, Retford (0777 860780)

Park near Sturton-le-Steeple church and walk past the pond, created by the Spadework project run by the County's Leisure Services. The pond has an island known as Edwin's Island, named after the JCB driver who worked on the project. At the crossroads, go ahead along Springs Lane, where a path of stone slabs lead you past a delightful waterside garden. After about three quarters of a mile, ignore the bridleway on the right but soon swing right under the railway bridge. There are wide verges and neat hedges on the lane leading uphill, High House Road. Though only 200 feet high, there are wide views, with South Wheatley to the north and Lincoln cathedral visible to the east if the air is clear. Less

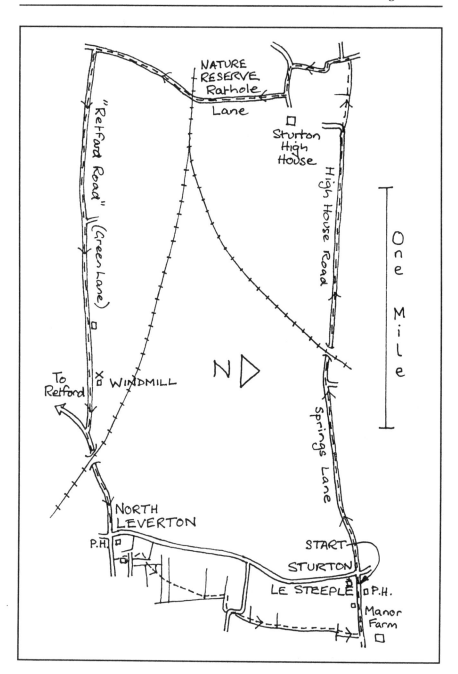

attractive though necessary are the three power stations on the banks of the Trent.

The lane curves left, but our route is ahead along the Trent Valley Way. Go through the hand gate and follow the edge of two fields, using the gates provided, to Blue Stocking Lane. Turn left and follow the lane to join Whinleys Road. A left turn here for a few yards, then right into Rathole Lane. At the foot of the hill, beside the level crossing is a nature reserve in the care of the Nottinghamshire Wildlife Trust. The reserve owes its existence to the tunnel and cutting excavated for the Retford-Gainsborough railway in 1849. The spoil was piled up nearby and has developed naturally into rough woodland rich in wild flowers.

Cross the railway line, watching out for coal trains en route for West Burton Power Station, and continue up hill beside woodlands. On your right you will pass the High Point Surge Vessel. This enigmatic construction would make a good subject for "Call My Bluff". In fact it is connected with a pipeline through which the fuel ash from Cottam power station, a very fine dust, is pumped to Sutton-cum-Lound. The ash is mixed with water and pumped as a slurry which is deposited in old sand and gravel workings. The tower contains valves which can be used to regulate the flow.

Turn left down Retford Gate, at first a grassy lane, then stone, then tarmac beyond the windmill. North Leverton Mill is one of only two working windmills in the county, and is open to the public. It was a subscription mill, built in 1813 for and by farmers in the local parishes to grind corn. The tower was raised to its present height in 1884. Since 1956 it has been run by a limited company, grinding grain and rolling or crushing oats and barley for animal feed. It is to the credit of local enthusiasts, some descended from its founders in 1813, that the mill has been preserved for us to enjoy.

Now called Mill Lane, our route joins a busy road, where you turn left along the pavement into North Leverton.

After pausing at the Royal Oak for refreshment, continue 200 yards along the Littleborough Road. A signpost on the left points to the church: the path passes left of the church, goes through a gap behind the churchyard and crosses a grassy lane. After crossing the stile, one should go to the middle of the field, then turn right to the corner and another stile.

Cross the grass field to a gate, then half-left across an arable field to a stile. Cross a narrow meadow, then continue to the corner of the next field. Cross the stile and follow the edge of another grass field to a double stile and footbridge with a Trent Valley Way sign. The route has been diverted here to the right around the field edge to a stile into Three Leys Lane. Turn left to another stile and continue to follow the right-hand boundary, watching out for rabbit-holes. A small grass field brings you to the Littleborough road, where turn left to return to your starting point and the Reindeer Inn.

North Leverton Windmill

16: CLARBOROUGH & HIGH HOUSE

This truly rural walk makes full use of the green lanes which link the Idle and Trent valleys and visits an unusual nature reserve.

Distance: 6 miles

Time: 3 hours

Start: Clarborough church, map reference SK 734833.

Maps: Pathfinder SK 68/78 (East Retford North), Landranger 120 (Mansfield & Worksop)

How to Get There:

By Car: Clarborough is on the A620 a couple of miles east of Retford

By Bus: Hourly services (95, 96, 97 or 98) between Retford and Gainsborough. Few buses on Sundays.

Refreshments: None

Nearest Tourist Information: Retford Tourist Information Service, Amcott House, 40 Grove Street, Retford (0777 860780)

Start the walk at Clarborough church, a 13th century building much restored in 1874. The churchyard contains a yew tree believed to be 1,000 years old. Walk up the lane to the left of the church lychgate, past the school and along a short green lane. Cross the stile on your left and head diagonally up the grass field, then along the edge of the next, a stiff little climb which brings you out near the junction of Howbeck Lane and Red Flats Lane. Turn right to follow the latter, which joins the intriguingly named Blue Stocking Lane, another attractive green lane, in a T-junction.

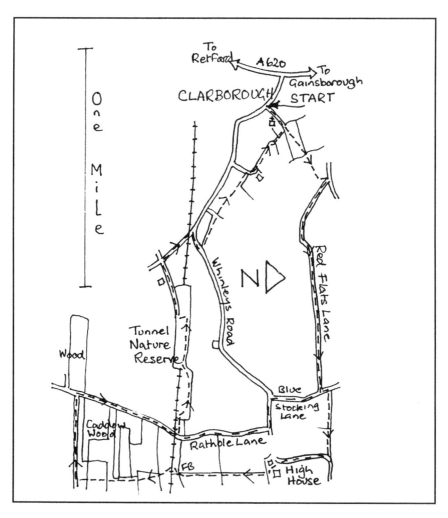

Turn left, then right along a bridleway leading along field edges to High House Road. Turn right and go ahead to pass to the right of the enormous farm buildings, then left at the end. Turn right to two gates, go through the left-hand one and straight down the hill to a substantial and very smart bridge. Angle right across rough pasture to a stile and cross the railway by the splendid white-painted board-walk to another stile. Now climbing, go slightly left across the first field to a double stile and continue up the next field to a stile 100 yards from the corner.

After a stretch of headland, cross a narrow field to reach Caddow Wood. Pass through the wood and go straight ahead to Retford Gate, a wide green lane. Turn right and at the top, right again to cross the railway once again at a level crossing. Just beyond is the entrance to Clarborough Nature Reserve, owned by the Nottinghamshire Wildlife Trust. Here once stood the crossing-keeper's cottage, as a few fruit-trees and garden plants testify. The reserve, acquired in 1971 by the Trust, is the result of earth excavated to create a cutting and tunnel in 1849. It has a variety of trees and flowers, which are open to the public at all times.

There is a straight path parallel with the railway, but the Trust have made a Trail through the trees, easy to follow and starting with some steps on the right. Continue near the right-hand edge of the reserve as far as the gate on the right, where turn left to cross the reserve and the railway beneath it. Now go to the right down a track: you may find some barbed wire but a hook at one end allows you to pass through.

Joining another lane, swing right to cross the railway again. Turn right for a few yards up the tarmac road, then left to cross a plank bridge, then a stile. The footpath crosses two grass fields, first skirting the woodland to a gate, then continuing parallel to the left-hand field boundary to reach the corner of a hedge and follow it to a stile in the corner. Now continue ahead past some light industrial units, through a ˜ gate and along the edge of an arable field to a stile just around the corner of the field. Across the foot of the meadow is a stile into the churchyard, and you have only to follow the path past the church to your starting point.

17: RETFORD & HAYTON

An excellent medium length walk along green lanes, good field paths and a delightful stretch of the Chesterfield Canal

Distance: 6 miles

Time: 3 hours

Start: In the layby near the Hop Pole public house, Retford, map reference SK 720818

Maps: Pathfinder SK 68/78 (East Retford), Landranger 120 (Mansfield and Worksop)

How to Get There:

By Car: The layby is on the A620, on the eastern fringe of Retford

By Bus: Hourly service between Retford and Gainsborough (95/96)

Refreshments: "Boat Inn", Hayton, "The Gate", Clarborough, "Hop Pole", Retford

Nearest Tourist Information: Retford Tourist Information Centre, Amcott House, 40, Grove Street, Retford (0777 860780)

The Chesterfield Canal, completed in 1777, was built to link Chesterfield with the river Trent at West Stockwith, and for many years did a roaring trade, mostly coal but also bricks, lead and corn. In the 1840's it was used to transport a quarter of a million tons of stone from Anston to build the Houses of Parliament. However the railways were soon to offer strong competition, and the collapse of the 3,000-yard long Norwood Tunnel in 1908 added to the commercial decline. Commercial traffic ended in 1956, but the canal still provides pleasure boating, a linear nature reserve, and a footpath passing through Worksop, Retford and many attractive villages.

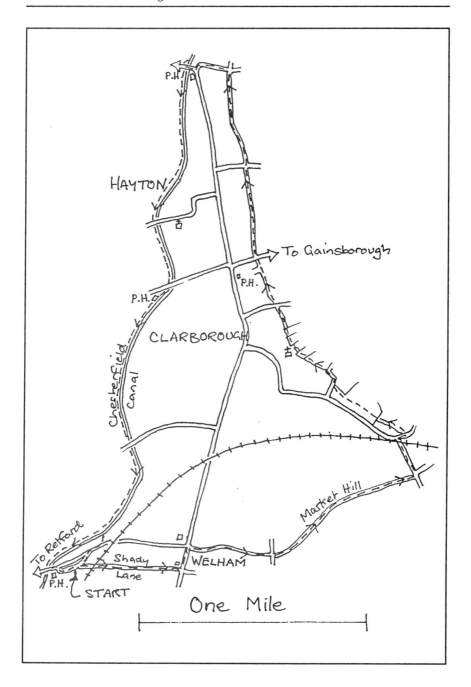

The walk starts just north of Retford on the Gainsborough road, just past the canal-side "Hop Pole" pub. Park in the lay-by. Follow the public footpath signposted from the lay-by to cross the railway and continue along Shady Lane to a street in the tiny village of Welham. Turn left, then right up a lane to a crossroad: continue ahead along a pleasant tree-lined green lane, turning left at the end.

Cross the railway again, then turn immediately right. A signpost on the left directs you along the top of a wood and through a gate. Go straight ahead and where the field narrows follow the right-hand hedge to the corner. Cross the stile and bear right along a track, passing through a gate near some light industrial buildings. Go forward to a stile, then along a field edge to another stile, which is around the corner of the field. Across the meadow is yet another stile into Clarborough churchyard.

A stone path takes you through the churchyard, and after crossing two stiles go straight ahead across two meadows and into an ancient lane. At the end, follow a headland then keep ahead to a road. After crossing, follow a hedged lane: keep straight on at the first cross-road, pass a farm gate and a stretch of sandstone track, then take the lane left. This brings you out on the main road beside the "Boat Inn", where you can quench your thirst and have a bite to eat if wished.

Cross the bridge and go left along the canal towpath. After a mile, at Clarborough Top Bridge, you will find the "Gate" public house, a peaceful place at the edge of the village with a colony of the greediest ducks ever seen. At the next bridge is Bonemill Farm, where bones were ground –probably by a horse driving the grindstone – to make fertiliser. Its building coincided with the arrival of the canal in 1775.

Just beyond the Bonemill Farm is Well House, where a spring known as Saint John's Well was famed for its beneficial effects for those with rheumatic complaints. In 1750 John Hutchinson built a bath-house there and tried to popularise it as a Spa, but without success.

Next you arrive at Whitsunday Pie Lock, the highest wide lock on the canal. It appears that the navvies finished building this lock on Whit Sunday, and a local farmer's wife baked a huge pie for them to mark the occasion. You can either cross the bridge below the lock and cross the road to your starting point, or continue to the next bridge and return via the "Hop Pole".

Whitsundaypie Lock

18: RETFORD & BABWORTH

Three miles of the Chesterfield canal and a splendid section of Green Mile Lane make this an easy walk to enjoy. Babworth church, without its association with the Pilgrim Fathers, would still be a lovely church in a splendid setting, and should be seen at bluebell time.

Distance: 8 miles

Time: 4 hours

Start: From the ASDA store in Retford, map reference SK 703808

Maps: Pathfinders SK 68/78 (East Retford North) and SK 67/77 (Clumber Park), Landranger 120 (Mansfield & Worksop)

How to Get There:

By Car: Retford is at the junction of the A620 and A638

By Bus: Most bus services in the area start at or pass through Retford

By Train: Retford is on the main East Coast line

Refreshments: None on the route, plenty of choice in Retford. No shortage of picnic spots on the route

Nearest Tourist Information: Retford Tourist Information Centre, Amcott House, 40 Grove Street, Retford (0777 860780)

Coming out of the store, turn left to a side road and left again to a hump-backed bridge. To the left can be seen a tiny aqueduct which carries the Chesterfield canal across the River Idle. Walk ahead through part of King's Park to the canal, your path shaded by Lombardy poplars. The park, 45 acres of parkland and riverside walks, was opened in 1938 to commemorate the coronation of George VI.

Climb down the steps to the canal, turn right and walk away from the centre of town. Whereas many towns line their canal with warehouses

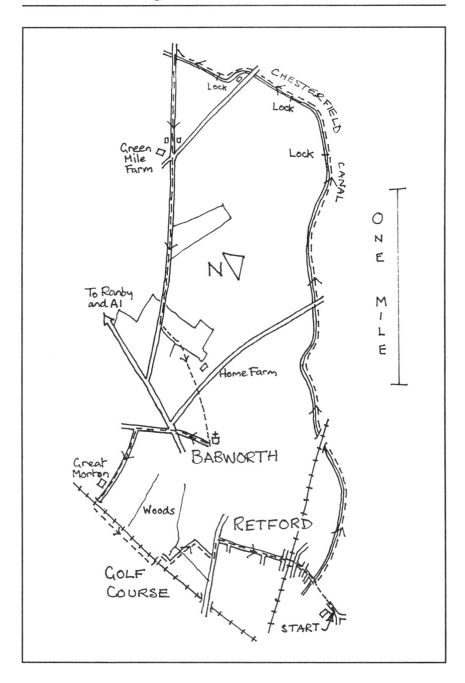

Babworth Church

and factories, this is a green, tree-lined route, passing West Retford lock, an attractive cemetery and a hospital grounds. Town ducks sidle up looking for tidbits. As you leave the town behind, casual strollers thin out, though fishermen can be found anywhere. Occasionally a narrow-boat burbles past, either upstream towards the head of navigation at Worksop, or down towards the junction with the Trent at West Stock-with.

Following the canal for three miles we pass through quiet farmland and encounter the four Forest Locks, formerly known as Sherwood Forest Locks as they were just inside the boundary of the royal forest. The canal is crossed by the Old London Road, which carried the Great North Road until a couple of hundred years ago when a diversion took traffic through Retford. This seemed like a good idea at the time.

After the top lock, leave the canal at bridge 52, where a fine grove of beech trees guards Green Mile Lane. Cross the bridge and follow the lane for over a mile. The first section has been planted with a variety of attractive trees and shrubs which are a credit to its landowner, while beyond the first road you continue along a wide green lane. Just after passing between woodland on both sides, turn left to head straight for Babworth.

Follow the grassy path until it bends, then cross a tiny patch of parkland with a handful of oaks on the right and continue through meadowland to a road. The path continues clearly marked across arable land, and only at the last minute is there a glimpse of the eighteenth century Babworth Hall before the path slips past the ha-ha to the church.

There was already a hall here in the 13th century, but it was in 1715 that John Simpson transformed it in the Queen Anne style. Only a third of that fine house remains now. In the 19th century the hall and park were considerably improved and the grounds landscaped by Humphrey Repton. This meant clearing away cottages and a windmill and diverting the Retford to Worksop road, which had passed close to the church. There was also a fine lake which has completely dried up.

A plaque placed in the church porch by the General Society of Mayflower Descendants tells us that the Rev. Richard Clayton became the minister here in 1586. A Separatist, he wished to purge the church of

Romish attributes like the hierarchy of clergy and ornate clerical vestments. As rector, he befriended and counselled William Brewster, Master of the King's Post at Scrooby and William Bradford of Austerfield, who walked 9 miles to his church every Sunday. Both of them were to be Governors of Plymouth, New England. Clayton was deprived of his position at Babworth in 1605, went to Scrooby and from there to Amsterdam. The Separatists moved on to Leyden and eventually to Plymouth and the New World.

On leaving the church, follow the drive to the A620 passing the Old Vicarage, now known as Haygarth House. This impressive building was rebuilt in the 19th century by the Rev. Bridgeman Simpson, who also refurbished the church. His rectory was so grandiose that succeeding parsons could not afford to live there and a new rectory was built up the road.

Cross the A620 and go along the road opposite, signposted Apley Head and Clumber. Follow the footpath on the right hand side, where wild privet scents the air in summer, as far as a bridleway on the left. This is the surfaced drive to Great Morton Farm, a neat, attractive house which you pass to reach a tunnel under a railway. Turn left immediately along a farm track which brings you to woodlands and the 15th tee of the Retford Golf Club. Take care not to disturb the players, who have not yet discovered the secret of walking without also carrying lots of heavy equipment and attacking a small white ball.

Keep to the edge of the fairway to a bridge on the left which must be a candidate for the world's longest footbridge. Cross the railway and follow a path half-right which cuts off a corner of a wood. Cross a track and go around two sides of the playing-field to reach Ordsall Road. Turn left for 50 yards, then right along the tree-lined Ordsall Park Road. After crossing a massive railway footbridge, this time over the main East Coast line, keep straight ahead along a leafy lane and Pelham Road. Just ahead is a bridge over the canal, and you retrace your steps to ASDA.

19: RANBY & SCOFTON

Any walk involving the Chesterfield Canal can't be bad, but farm roads across the Osberton estate and the lovely Green Mile Lane complete a circuit which is pleasant in any season and idyllic on a summer's day

Distance: 7.5 miles

Time: 3.5 hours

Start: Ranby's village hall, map reference SK 649813

Maps: Pathfinder SK 68/78 (East Retford), Landranger 120 (Mansfield & Worksop)

How to Get There:

By Car: Ranby is just off the A1,, and the Village Hall is right opposite the northernmost entry to the village.

By Bus: Hourly service 42 between Retford and Worksop, Monday to Saturday

Refreshments: "Chequers Inn", Ranby

Nearest Tourist Information: Either Worksop or Retford

Pass the front door of the hall (marked 1927) to join the Chesterfield Canal and turn left along the tow-path. This is a delightful stretch of canal, with willows bowed over the opposite bank and after the bend, woodland on your left. Watch out for squirrels here, and possibly frogs too. At bridge 52, edge left through a grove of stately beech to join Green Mile Lane, which runs between hedges and well-established oak and sweet chestnut trees. Turn left along the lane and follow it for about a mile. To your right there will be glimpses of Ranby Hall, a late 18th century house built around an earlier core. Past some neat cottages and Low Farm: the lane narrows as you approach the A1.

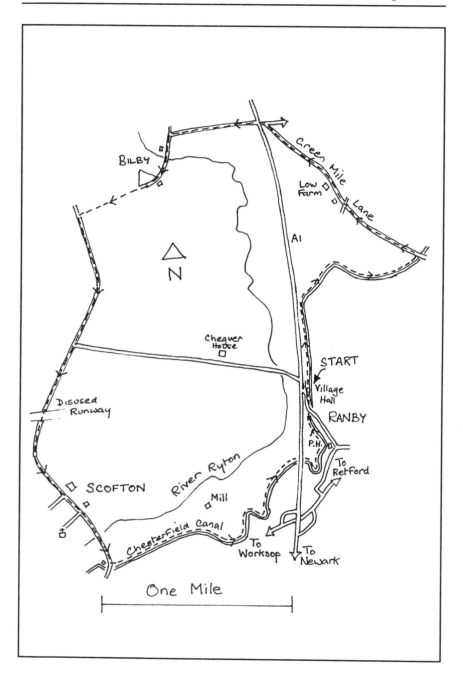

One Mile

Standing at a cross-roads, take great care negotiating the dual carriage-way and enter the lane opposite which in half a mile reaches Bilby, turning left at a T-junction. Bilby is a scattering of houses around a bridge over the river Ryton, a pleasant spot to linger in Spring as ducks and geese paddle in the river and daffodils and bluebells fringe the beech-wood beyond it.

Here there stood a Hall where the Foljambe family lived during alterations to Osberton Hall at the end of the 19th century. Bilby Hall was then demolished and converted to keepers' cottages and kennels.

Past the wood, follow the track to a T-junction, then turn left between hawthorn hedges. After passing through a shelter belt of Scots Pine the track passes between mature oaks with outriders of pine and thorn, then enters pig country.

On either side sows of impressive size roam among their simple shelters, their beady stare reinforcing the "Keep Out" notices. A lane on the left signed "Barnby Moor 1 mile" could reduce your walk to 5 miles. Continuing the walk, you are now following a tarmac track with wide verges, passing a fir plantation, then running between tall hawthorn hedges with newly planted lime and spiny robinias. Next, a reminder of World War II as you cross the airstrip. This was laid as a satellite for RAF Finningley as a Bomber Command airfield. Subsequently it became an Advanced Flying School where flying instructors were trained. It was derequisitioned in 1960.

Descend through a wide avenue of oaks to Scofton, the heart of the Osberton Estate. A signpost opposite Grange Farm points the way to the church, which is worth a detour. Then pass a Victorian letter-box, another bridge over the Ryton, a lake which once served as mill-pond, and distant views right of the Hall.

Reaching the canal, admire the lock to the right but turn left to follow the grassy tow-path back to Ranby, with no company but swans, ducks, Canada geese and coots for well over a mile. As you pass the Chequers Inn, make a note to return for refreshment, as your starting point is another half mile. In case of extreme thirst, of course, you can leave the canal at bridge 51! Otherwise, you need only follow the canal to your starting point.

20: KILTON & SCOFTON

A walk from the fringe of Worksop along the Chesterfield canal to the Osberton estate and one of the prettiest stretches of canal-side scenery.

Distance: 5 miles

Time: 2.5 hours

Start: The Bracebridge Centre in Bracebridge Avenue, Kilton, SK 596792

Maps: Pathfinders SK 47/57 (Staveley) and 67/77 (Clumber Park, Landranger 120 (Mansfield and Worksop)

How to Get There:

By Car: The Bracebridge Centre is one mile east of the centre of Worksop, off the B6079

By Bus: Frequent service number 44 from Worksop

Refreshments: None

Nearest Tourist Information: Worksop Tourist Information Centre, Public Library, Memorial Avenue, Worksop (0909 501148)

Walk past the Bracebridge Centre on the left-hand side and turn left along the bank of the Chesterfield canal. The canal swings right to cross the river Ryton, then left again. For a mile or so the canal runs beside the river, while to the right there is a sports field and a couple of commercial buildings. Far right can be seen the headstock and plant of Manton colliery, which was sunk in 1907, its spoil-heap now grassed over.

When you have crossed the board-walk over a canal overflow, then passed bridge 45 (1929), the fringes of Worksop are left behind. A tall railway viaduct crosses the canal and river, then the canal heads straight for Scofton and the Osberton Estate. Just before the next bridge, the high hedges on the left give way to an oak wood. Number 46 is a roving bridge, where the towpath changes sides and a horse could cross the canal to the opposite side without unhitching the tow-rope.

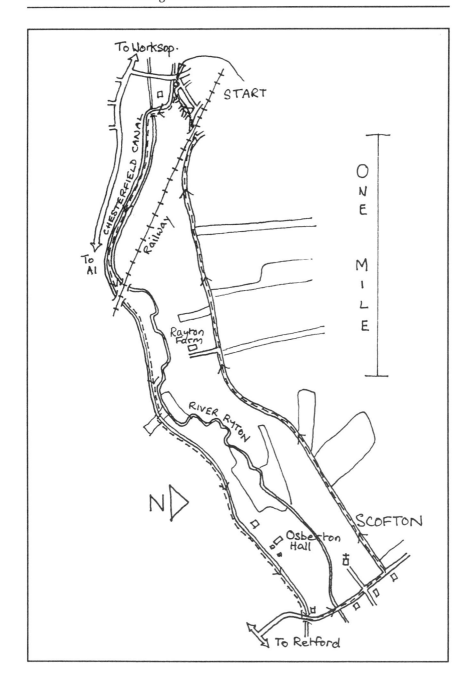

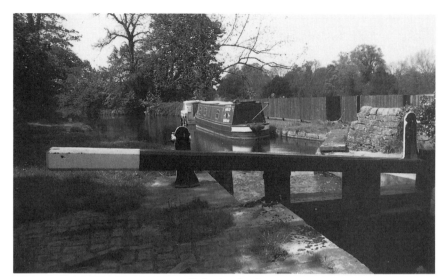

Osberton Lock

As you approach the heart of the estate there is a fir plantation on the right, then parkland which surrounds Osberton Hall, a beautiful setting only slightly marred by modern farm buildings. Beyond the Hall there is a view of the stables and a curious hexagonal tower, then an attractive tree-lined section of the canal, popular with the more discerning fishermen. A lock and the lock-keeper's cottage mark the end of the canal-side walk: turn left along the road into Scofton, with lime-trees on either side.

A sign on the left points to the church, which was built in 1833 at the site of Scofton Hall. The Foljambe family had acquired Scofton a few years previously, and it was George Savile Foljambe who built the church in memory of his first wife.

Continue past the lane to the church to a sign which says "Rayton Lane $1^3/_4$". Here turn left to follow this track back to Kilton, with a fine view across parkland to Scofton church and the Hall. Tall trees shade the track as you pass the jumps used during the Osberton cross-country trials.

Continue straight ahead until, reaching another road, you turn left to pass under the railway, then left again along Bracebridge Avenue to your starting point.

21: NETHER LANGWITH

A walk in a heavily-wooded part of Nottinghamshire, right on the Derbyshire border. As in much of the coal country, the mines make little impact on the countryside. The paths are all well-used, not least because miners, more than any other workers, appreciate clean air and green landscapes.

Distance: 5 miles

Time: 2.5 hours

Start: In the layby near Langwith Mill, map reference SK 546792

Maps: Pathfinders SK 46/56 (Mansfield North) and SK 47/57 (Staveley), Landranger 120 (Mansfield and Worksop)

How to Get There:

By Car: The layby is half way between Cuckney and Nether Langwith on the A632

By Bus: Hourly services, 9 between Worksop and Mansfield and 10 between Ollerton and Mansfield

Refreshments: "Jug and Glass", Nether Langwith

Nearest Tourist Information: Worksop Tourist Information Centre, Public Library, Memorial Avenue, Worksop (0909 501148)

The cotton mill was built in 1760, powered by the river Poulter via a mile-long contoured canal from Langwith Lodge Lake. The mill was converted to mill corn in 1886. The Mill House, mainly Georgian with an older and a more modern wing, is now a restaurant. Follow the lane past the mill and Pasture Hill Farm and at the end continue along the field headland. Enter a meadow and cross it to the far corner. Here you enter a hedged lane, go up to join another, and turn left. Where this farm road swings left to Blue Barn Farm, pass through the kissing-gate ahead, go to the end of the meadow and left up the hill to join a lane.

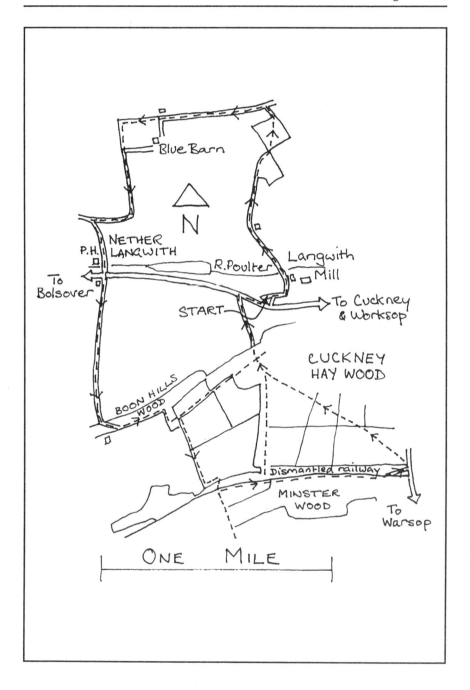

Follow the lane to a road and turn left past leafy gardens to the A632. On your right the shallow river Poulter runs between grassy banks and the "Jug and Glass" offers excellent refreshment. Cross the main road and follow a hedged lane which swings left at the end up a steep incline. At the top of the hill you will find a stile on your left, and a narrow path keeps to the edge of Boon Hills Wood. Turn right to follow the edge of the woodland, then sharp left to a stile. Here you may shorten your walk by going straight ahead as shown on the plan.

Our route turns right over a stile and along the edge of three fields. Turn left along the woodside for 60 yards, then right to climb stone steps and reach a disused railway track. As you turn left along the track, you may catch glimpses to the right of the ever-advancing spoil heap of Warsop Main pit.

At the next road, turn left for about 30 yards, then take the diagonal path across Cuckney Hay Wood, ignoring any side-tracks. At the far corner a narrow path slopes downhill, leaves the wood and is hedged as far as the road. Turn right to return to the start.

22: CUCKNEY & CHURCH WARSOP

Starting from the lovely village of Cuckney, the walk passes through a variety of woodland between the rivers Poulter and Meden

Distance: 7.5 miles

Time: 3.5 hours

Start: Cuckney church car park, map reference SK 566714

Maps: Pathfinder SK 47/57 (Staveley & Worksop) and SK 46/56 (Mansfield North)

How to Get There:

By Car: Cuckney is on the A60, 6 miles south of Worksop

By Bus: Service 32 Mansfield/Worksop hourly, but sketchy service on Sundays

Refreshments: "Greendale Oak", Cuckney

Nearest Tourist Information: Worksop Tourist Information Centre, Public Library, Memorial Avenue, Worksop (0909 501148)

Start at Cuckney church, which has a large car park. The churchyard of the 13th century church, perched above the river Poulter, extends over the site of Thomas de Cuckney's fortified 12th century manor house whose moat can still be seen. The church is also built over the mass grave of 200 men who must have fallen in battle near this spot. Notice the pinfold near the entrance to the car park: here the Pinder kept animals which had been found straying, until a fine had been paid.

Walk down Norton Road away from the village to a stile on the left, just past the river Poulter. Walk parallel to the river to a stile on the wooded

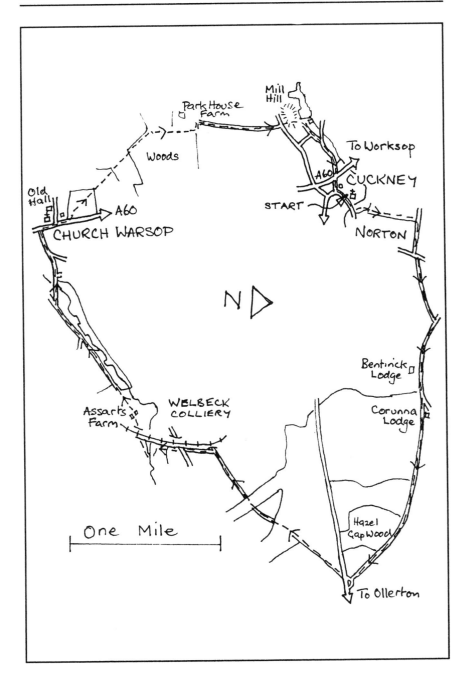

bank on the right. Enter the field and follow the right-hand edge to a road. Turn right to Norton village, then left and immediately right. A decorative notice-board at the cross-roads announces that the village has won the "Best Kept Village" competition four times. Follow the road for nearly a mile.

After passing an estate road on the left, the Welbeck Estate's Great Lake and Carburton Forge Dam can be seen. Buzzards are often sighted in woodland near the weir. Opposite Bentinck Lodge on the right is an impressive memorial to Lord George Bentinck, M.P. for King's Lynn, who died near this spot on the 21st of September 1848. A flattering quotation of Disraeli is carved on the pedestal. At Corunna Lodge angle right. The lodges belong to the Welbeck estate, former home of the Dukes of Portland.

The delightful woodland track runs for about a mile to Hazel Gap and the A616. At first the track passes between low sandstone cliffs, and sweet chestnut trees predominate in the path-side woods. There are conifers on the left, but screened by naturally spreading deciduous trees. Further on, as the lane widens out, there are beech, sycamore and oak to be seen. At Hazel Gap, where there is an unofficial car park for forest walkers, cross the road and go down the signposted path past sweet chestnut trees.

The path passes straight through part of Gleadthorpe Experimental Husbandry farm: leaving the woodlands, there is a view of Meden Vale mine ahead, and a gargantuan crop watering system can be seen in the adjacent field. On reaching a mineral railway coming from the mine just beyond, turn left here beside the embankment, cross the road and continue along a field edge. Enter the grass field beyond and continue to a stile and footbridge over the river Meden. The path then swings right, and there is a stile from the fenced path into the normally overgrown fringe of a field. Turn right and head for a tunnel under the railway.

Go straight on to Assarts Farm, whose name indicates that it was built on land cleared from Sherwood Forest. Pass between the buildings, turn right towards the farm and left along the drive. Soon you can see the twists and turns of the Meden in the trees to your right. Turn right opposite Burns Farm to cross a bridge over the Meden and keep left through a small estate. At the junction beside Manor Farm keep ahead.

To the left is Warsop Mill and the mill pond, but our route is right past the church.

Warsop Church

Basically a Norman church, Saint Peter and Paul's has been extended over the years and become an impressive building on its elevated site. In the thirties it was threatened by subsidence after the Staveley Coal and Iron Company had unwisely been given permission to mine beneath it, and it was the National Coal Board which later had to foot the bill for extensive repairs.

Behind the church on the Shirebrook road is the 14th century Manor House formerly known as Old Hall Farm, now a thriving community centre. Continue the walk up Cuckney Hill, turning left just behind the farmyard.

Cross a couple of fields diagonally and keep ahead to the corner of Oakfield Plantation. Go down the path just inside the wood, veer slightly right, then go left down a forest ride to join Park House Farm's access road. Follow this to the A632 and cross the road. Go over Mill Hill, once a pile of waste from the mill-pond but now a splendid beech wood. The mill itself, amputated of its upper storey, is now the village school. Toplis' Upper Mill, as it was called, was converted in 1785 from an existing building, with a wheel 22 feet in diameter and 12 feet wide. It was built in 1723 as a corn mill and converted to cotton about 1785.

Most of its workers were pauper children, mainly from the London area. Between 1786 and 1802 seven hundred children, some as young as five, were apprenticed. About a third were passed on to other work, while of those who remained, six per cent died and eighteen per cent sensibly absconded.

As you go along School Lane and cross carefully to go straight along Creswell Road, you pass houses used to lodge the "apprentices" and other workers. Baker's Row is the first on the left, then on Creswell road Maltkin Row (a reminder of Cuckney's hop-growing era), Parker's Row and Ten Row, which now has less that ten houses due to the widening of the A60.

Cross the main road with great care to reach the "Greendale Oak", a pub named after an enormous tree on the Welbeck estate. The Second Duke of Portland bet in 1724 that a carriage and six could drive through it, and cut an opening through the tree to win his wager. The tree did not long survive the experience. To reach your starting point, turn left just beyond the pub.

The "Greendale Oak" has bar meals at lunch times Monday to Saturday, with only three-course lunches on Sunday. Restaurant meals are on offer in the evenings, Sunday excepted.

23: CLUMBER & CROOKFORD

The National Trust's Clumber Park is its only property in Nottinghamshire, but with four thousand acres of forest, six hundred acres of grassland heath, farmland and pleasure gardens it is enormously popular for walking, fishing, and the quiet enjoyment of its thriving wildlife. An easy-to-follow walk skirts the lake which is the heart of Clumber and extends to visit the delightful Crookford Water.

Distance: 9 miles – could be split into two shorter walks

Time: 4.5 hours

Start: Clumber Park lakeside car park, map reference SK 539744

Maps: Pathfinder SK 67/77 (Clumber Park), Landranger 120 (Mansfield & Worksop)

How to Get There:

By Car: Clumber Park is 4 miles west of Worksop via the A57

Refreshments: Clumber tea-room

Nearest Tourist Information: Worksop Tourist Information Centre, Public Library, Memorial Avenue, Worksop (0909 501148)

Park in the main lakeside car park. This will involve a charge for non-members of the National Trust. Near here the ducks, swans and Canada geese have learned to expect a snack, and will complain if you forget to bring them one. Just beyond the car park you will find the site of Clumber House, whose walls are marked out in the turf. It was built in 1767 for the Duke of Newcastle by Stephen Wright, and was demolished just before World War Two. If the house has gone, there are still outbuildings ranged beside the Old Turning Yard, containing a restaurant and tea-room and the inevitable shop. Beyond them is the Victorian Gothic chapel, built in 1889 of white Steetley stone with red facings.

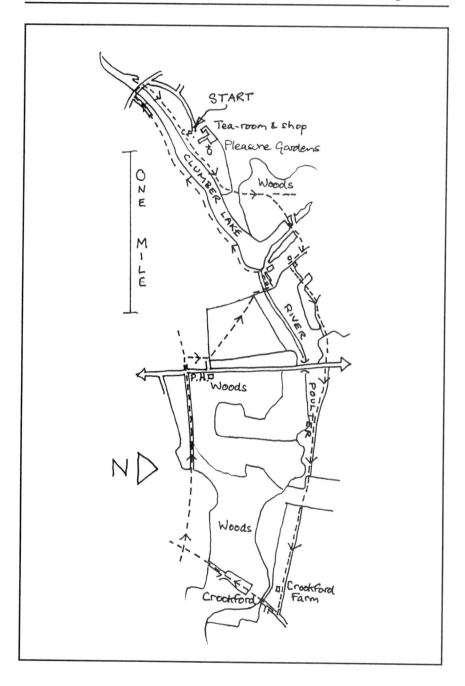

Passing the chapel, walk through the Pleasure Gardens. You have a choice of routes, along the Lincoln Terrace beside the lake or through the 24 acres of grassy glades and specimen trees. At the end of the gardens, cross to Ash Hill Wood, a 70-acre plantation. Scots pine, larch, birch and sycamore were first planted in 1934. Pass through the wood to reach the end of an arm of the lake.

Join a surfaced road and follow it to a T-junction, where you turn right past a terrace of workers' cottages built in the 19th century for the estate staff. With their steep roofs and enormous chimneys these houses dominate Hardwick village. Take the bridleway on the left. This leads past a fruit farm and through woodland to the A614: cross this with great care and follow the track beside the river Poulter.

The track crosses farmland to reach Cross Lane. Turn right to reach the ford at Crookford water, a pleasant spot for a picnic, "coffee-stop" or just a contemplative paddle. Cross the footbridge, follow the track through a sandy glade and leave the track to go straight ahead to the double electricity poles. Follow the row of poles through the wood and across an arable field to West Drayton Avenue. Turn right and follow this lane through Normanton Larches, which despite its name has a rich variety of mature deciduous trees.

On reaching the A614 again, cross to the Drayton Gate, enter the park and turn right to reach the estate road near the Normanton Gate. Turn a few yards right and pass through a bridlegate on the left. The corner to corner bridleway provides a good view of Hardwick village, the original 18th-century village for estate workers, the weir and the tree-fringed lake. Cross the river Poulter by the bridge beside the ford, said to be the longest in the County, pass Hardwick Grange and swing left to the lakeside. The 87-acre lake and its environs have played host to over 130 different species of birds in recent years.

Cross the weir, recently refurbished by British Coal following mining subsidence, and follow the path along the lakeside. There are ever-changing views across the water to the forests, pleasure gardens and buildings, and on this side you will meet a "Greek" temple contemporary with the house. Continue to Carburton bridge, another of Stephen Wright's creations, cross it and follow the edge of the lake through Nursery Wood to rediscover the car park.

24: ELKESLEY & BOTHAMSALL

A walk around the northern limits of Sherwood Forest, visiting Conjure Alders, where two rivers meet, then separate again, and the delightful Crookford Water.

Distance: 8 miles

Time: 4 hours

Start: Elkesley village hall car park, map reference SK 688755

Maps: Pathfinder Sk 67/77 (Clumber Park), Landranger 120 (Mansfield and Worksop)

How to Get There:

By Car: Elkesley is just off the A1,, 3 miles south of its junction with the A57

By Bus: Occasional service (35) between Retford and Ollerton and 38, two hourly, between Retford and Newark

Refreshments: "Normanton Inn", near Drayton Gate and "Robin Hood", Elkesley

Nearest Tourist Information: Retford Tourist Information Centre, Amcott House, 40, Grove Street, Retford (0777 860780)

The walk begins in the pleasant village of Elkesley, which turns its back on the nearby A1. Near the church is the Village Hall, where we start our walk by strolling past the sports pitches and out into Brough Lane. Turn right along the lane, then left as signposted down to the river Poulter, with a fine view of woodland beyond. Cross the bridge and follow a splendid grassy track through Elkesley Wood. Arrows keep you left at two path junctions, then right to leave the wood beside the beautifully-tended "Beggars Rest".

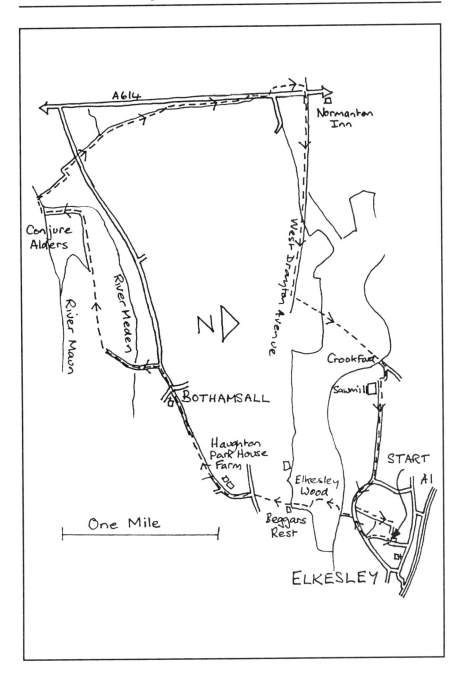

Continue along the track to West Drayton Avenue, with its row of tall trees. This avenue, also known as Duke's Drive, was designed as a grand approach to Clumber Park from the Great North Road, a distance of 3 miles. The trees were planted in the eighteen-twenties.

Cross the road to enter some farm gates and pass Haughton Park House Farm, continuing past the front of the graceful house with its white wooden cupola. It was built in 1700 and restored in 1940. The lane past the farm brings you into Bothamsall beside the church: a tiny village winding its way past its Victorian church, it was part of the Duke of Newcastle's estate. It is a pleasure to walk straight ahead through the village where each house is neat, trim, and usually awash with flowers. Near the end of the village a lane goes steeply left down to the river Meden and crosses it.

If you look up to the right you will see, at the west end of the village, a clump of trees marking the motte and bailey of Bothamsall Castle, believed to be of Norman origin. Continue along the track to Conjure Alders, where the rivers Maun and Meden join forces, but only for a

Footbridge near Elkesley

hundred yards, as they separate again for a few miles before they both join the river Idle. Alder trees, it is said, like their feet wet, so this area is ideal for them.

After crossing a footbridge over the river Maun, turn right to the next one over the Maun/Meden and cross this too. You are now following a bridleway which hugs the field edges as far as a road, then continues for about half a mile before it almost merges with the A614. Turn left here as waymarked, but don't join the road, as a narrow path runs through the ferns bordering the road for another half mile. You are obliged to join the road just short of a junction signposted "Bothamsall".

Angle across the road to the layby opposite and enter the woods beside a bridleway sign. However, don't follow the bridleway, but take the permissive footpath which swings right through oak-woods bordering the National Trust's Clumber Park estate, keeping parallel to the road as far as the Drayton Gate into the park.

Turn right here, cross the main road and follow the path ahead through enchanting deciduous woodland, with oak, sweet and horse chestnuts, sycamore and birch in abundance. After half a mile or so the path becomes a farm track passing through part of the Nottinghamshire oilfield: until recently "nodding donkeys" pumped oil beside the track. Turn left along a row of electricity poles to reach a strip of woodland bordering the river Poulter. On reaching a sandy clearing with a scattering of silver birch, keep right along the edge to the bridge and ford at Crookford.

Over the bridge, take the tarmac road on the right and just before the sawmill, take the path to the left. Pass the sawmill and continue to a junction: here turn right along Brough Lane. Almost opposite the path you first descended to the Poulter is a clear field-edge path leading you back to your starting-point.

25: BOTHAMSALL & CONJURE ALDERS

Successive overlords have left their mark on this peaceful corner of rural Nottinghamshire, and the walk encompasses two Norman castles, a King's ford and the site of a ducal family's ancestral home.

Distance: 6 miles

Time: 3 hours

Start: Bothamsall church, map reference SK 875734

Maps: Pathfinder SK 67/77 (Clumber Park & East Markham), Landranger 120 (Mansfield & Worksop)

How to Get There:

By Car: Bothamsall can be reached from the A1, or the A614 just north of Ollerton

By Bus: Occasional service (35) from Retford or Ollerton

Refreshments: With a detour, the "Red Lion", Walesby

Start the walk at Bothamsall church, which was erected by the Duke of Newcastle in the 19th century. Some of the stone came from Worksop Manor, which was then being demolished. Go along the narrow lane at the north side of the church, a pretty lane leading to a grassy farm track. The track leads to Haughton Park House, a fine building dating from 1700 with a distinctive cupola. Take the drive on the right down to a road, cross it and continue along the approach to Haughton Hall Farm. Here there are neat cottages and a massive brick building surmounted by a curious octagonal tower. This is in fact a grain store, but the builder clearly had in mind the view from the top, which is fenced around with a guard-rail.

Haughton Park House

This is the site, beside the river Maun, of the great house of the Holles family, destined to become Dukes of Newcastle with a new house in Clumber Park. Built in 1545 for Sir William Holles, master baker and Lord Mayor of London, and surrounded by a deer park and pleasure grounds, it was destroyed in 1770. By 1690, when the earl of Clare married the heiress of the Second Duke of Newcastle, the family had paid £10,000 for a barony and £5,000 for an earldom. A farmhouse on part of the site came to an abrupt end in 1943 when a fully-loaded Wellington bomber landed on it.

Cross the river Maun and follow the track left, then right at a junction. The track passes through a spinney and swings left again. Do not cross the stream, but turn right over the stile and follow the stream to the end of the field. Turn right here along the edge: the path becomes a farm track which swings left, heading for Walesby.

At this point, before turning left, look at the wooded area ahead. Shown on the map as Haughton Decoy, it was originally the site of a Norman motte and bailey castle, the mound being about 35 feet high and 40 feet

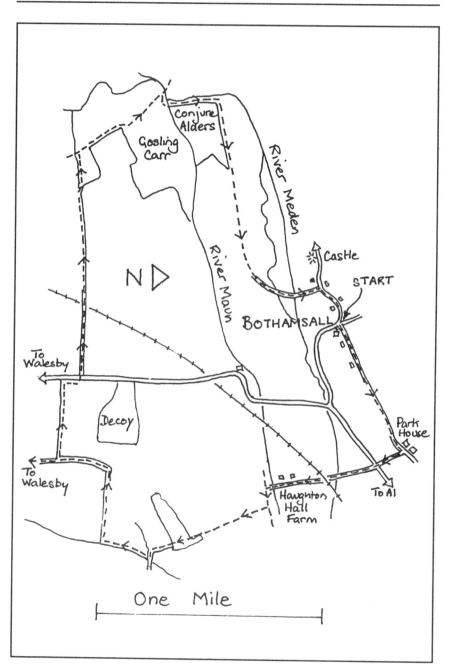

in diameter. In 1709 the site was in use as a duck decoy, in which wild ducks were driven into a narrowing channel to be shot by alleged sportsmen. The present owner intends to preserve the decoy as a wildlife reserve.

Continue to the point where you are about to pass under electricity transmission lines. Here your route continues through the gap right. For refreshments, go on for half a mile along Green Lane to Walesby: a right, then a left turn lead to the "Red Lion".

If spurning the fleshpots of Walesby, continue after the right turn to a road, turning right inside the field to a signpost. Cross Retford Road and enter a narrow path between a hedge and a fence. After crossing a mineral railway go ahead on a sandy farm track: on your right conifers compete with young oaks. At the end of this large field bear right, then left to follow the path at the edge of a conifer plantation.

On the left is Walesby Common, spared by the Forestry Commission and intensively used by the Scout movement. On joining another track bear right past conifers, then oak and birch scrub. Ignoring woodland rides left and right where your track double bends, continue through pines interspersed with sweet chestnut. The path narrows as it enters the low-lying borders of the river Maun, passing a planting of poplars.

As you reach the river beside a bridge it might be more accurate to call it a double river, for at this point the rivers Maun and Meden join, then separate again. Here was the "King's Ford", a crossing point used by the King when following the border of his forest. Turning right at the first bridge, pass the spillway through which the Meden is herded and cross the second bridge to walk beside it. This place is called Conjure Alders, for alder trees, which like to get their feet wet, grow in abundance beside both rivers.

Follow the track which bends right alongside the woodland and continues across the sandy plain. Where the track swings left towards Bothamsall there is a fine view of Bothamsall Castle, a small motte and bailey which may occupy an older site. Over to the right the headstocks of the showpiece Bevercotes Colliery are only partly screened by the woodland which surrounds them. On reaching the main street opposite a decorative range of 19th century cottages, turn right to pass through this very pleasant village and return to the church.

26: WEST MARKHAM

In the area known as the Dukeries, rarely-visited monuments can be found to the noble families who lived here, as well as some excellent walks. A grandiose mausoleum, an unusual parish church and a ruined chapel figure in this ramble.

Distance: 6 miles

Time: 3 hours

Start: West Markham church, map reference SK 722726

Maps: Pathfinder SK 66/67 (Clumber Park), Landranger 120

(Mansfield & the Dukeries)

How to Get There:

By Car: West Markham is just off the old North Road, now the B1164, a couple of miles north of Tuxford

By Bus: None

Refreshments: Royal Oak, West Markham

Nearest Tourist Information: Retford Tourist information Centre, Amcott House, 40 Grove Street, Retford (0777 860780)

Start the walk at West Markham church, walking between the east end of the church and the former village school to follow a narrow, high-hedged lane up to the former Great North Road. Turn left down hill to the Royal Oak, but turn left again just before the pub. A bridleway follows the hedge to a footbridge, then continues along a field boundary to join the farm track into Milton village.

Straight ahead can be seen the headstocks of Bevercotes colliery, which are rarely out of sight during the walk. This showpiece of the East

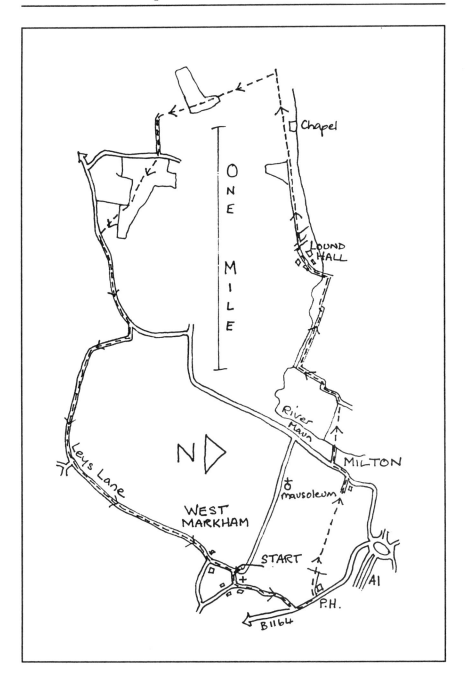

Midlands coalfield was opened in 1964. More attractive and certainly more remarkable is the classical building on the skyline to the left. The Church of All Saints was designed by Sir Robert Smirke, architect of the British Museum, for the fourth Duke of Newcastle as a mausoleum to house the tomb of his Duchess, who had died in 1822. The mausoleum was also to be the new parish church, but the villagers reverted to the old building as soon as they could, after the 8th Duke sold his estates in 1948. An avenue of lime trees still links the two churches.

On reaching Milton, turn left for a hundred yards, then right down a short lane to the river Maun. Cross the bridge and cross the meadow to a gate in the left-hand corner, with the village cricket pitch just to your left. Here you enter a fenced path, which you follow to the left. Eventually the path crosses a footbridge over a wide drainage ditch and joins a broad grass track: soon afterwards, at a T-junction, turn left to recross the tree-lined Maun.

Keep right past the building in front of you, which is an outbuilding of Lound Hall. The hall itself, which is now just on your right, was rebuilt in 1937 for the Peake family, a substantial neo-Georgian creation built of hand-made red brick. It is now maintained by British Coal as a training centre. Until recently it was the National Mining Museum, but its exhibits have now gone elsewhere. After passing the hall and crossing a road, keep ahead along a short lane, across a stile and along a pleasant grass strip which becomes a farm road.

On the right, an old chapel can soon be seen on the banks of the river Maun. It was built in the early 12th century, and was dedicated to Saint James. It became the chapel of the Stanhope and Holles families in Tudor times, but was abandoned when later generations of the family built on a grander scale at Clumber. Only fragments of the nave, chancel and north chantry remain, surrounded by trees and kamikaze nettles. Soon after passing the chapel, and with the grain store of Old Hall Farm in view to the right, take the track left. When this joins a road, go through the gate opposite and head over the shoulder of the hill before you. Crossing land used for motocross racing, keep left of a fence and shortly cross it by a stile. Head half-left across the field, turn left along the road, the after a quarter of a mile turn right beside two "nodding donkeys", a reminder that oil as well as coal lie beneath us.

Follow this pleasant green lane, keeping left at two junctions, to return to West Markham. The church is straight ahead, and merits a visit; every age and style of church architecture is to be seen, though its half-timbered gable and weatherboarded turret are unique in this area. From the churchyard, evidence can be seen in the grass field opposite of a deserted mediaeval village.

The ruins of Haughton Chapel

27: TUXFORD & EAST MARKHAM

A rural walk on the southern border of Bassetlaw. It is mostly on field paths and bridleways and the soil can be heavy, so it is advisable to set off in dry weather.

Distance: 7 miles

Time: 3.5 hours

Start: Near the "Fountain Inn" beside the railway bridge, map reference SK 717714.

Maps: Pathfinder SK 67/77 (Clumber Park), Landranger 120 (Mansfield & Worksop)

How to Get There:

By Car: Tuxford is just off the A1, 14 miles north of Newark, and the starting point is half a mile along the A6075 Darlton road.

By Bus: Frequent services 37, 37A and 38 Retford-Newark, a few buses on Sundays

Refreshments: "Fountain Inn", Tuxford. Nothing on the route, but a small detour is possible to one of the two East Markham pubs.

Nearest Tourist Information: Retford Tourist Information Centre, Amcott House, 40 Grove Street, Retford (0777 860780)

Start at the railway bridge half a mile east of Tuxford on the Darlton Road, Walk back towards Tuxford and cross the stile on the right opposite Faraday Avenue. Cross the meadow to a bridge, turn left at the edge of an arable field for 50 yards, then right up the field to join a track. Follow this left behind spacious gardens until the track joins a road.

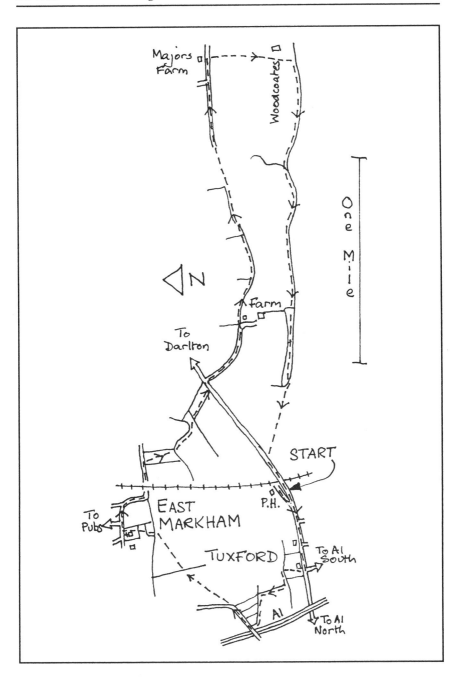

Turn right along the road to a signpost just beyond the houses. A very well-used path heads diagonally across two arable fields, heading for East Markham church. Cross a stile and a footbridge, pass a little paddock and climb up to the churchyard. The area behind the church is the site of a deserted mediaeval village, probably abandoned after the plague of 1605. Peaceful and well-tended, the churchyard is a good place to stand and enjoy.

East Markham Church

Saint John the Baptist church is a fine specimen of the Perpendicular architecture of the early 15th century. In the chancel is the alabaster table tomb of Judge Markham, who drew up the document for deposing Richard II. Nearby to the left is the Manor, built in the mid-17th century on the site of the house owned by the Markham family. Pass through the churchyard and turn right along the street, then right again to follow a lane and pass under a railway bridge. Just before the bridge a path runs beside the railway which, though unofficial, is very well used and leads to the start of the walk.

Beyond the bridge 150 yards, go right through the signposted gate and head for the left-hand corner of the field. Cross the stile and go left along the field-edge, then angle left to a bridge. Go up the field edge to a road, and enter the farm drive almost opposite. Follow this until it swings right, where continue ahead along a bridleway, passing through two gateways.

Soon after the second gateway, swing right into the adjoining field and follow the same line as before to join a hedged lane. Keep ahead on joining a road and after 100 yards turn right along a farm track opposite some farm buildings. Pass through a gate and follow the track, but turn right before the next gate, crossing a stile and plank bridge. Follow the left-hand field boundary to a dyke, cross a plank bridge: continue left at the edge of two arable fields, then a series of meadows.

In the last meadow cross the stile near the corner. The path should be clearly marked across the final arable field, but don't count on it. Reaching the road, turn left to your starting point. The Fountain pub provides refreshment.

Some headland paths on this walk have been illegally ploughed out for at least 10 years. Readers would do their bit to improve our footpaths by reporting further transgressions to the Rights of Way Officer at Trent Bridge House, West Bridgford.

28: HEADON & GROVE

*A truly rural walk between isolated villages in the rolling countryside
south-east of Retford*

Distance: 7.5 miles

Time: 3.5 hours

Start: Headon village hall, map reference SK 749771

Maps: Pathfinder SK 67/77 (Clumber Park), Landranger 120 (Mansfield
and Worksop)

How to Get There:

By Car: Headon is 4 miles south-east of Retford along minor roads

By Bus: Service 37/37a Retford to Newark about every two hours,
Monday to Saturday

Refreshments: "Duke William", Askham and Grove Garden Centre

Nearest Tourist Information: Retford Tourist Information Centre,
Amcott House, 40, Grove Street, Retford (0777 860780)

Park at Headon village hall. Walk downhill and turn left as signposted
opposite the churchyard. Pass the cottages and keep ahead, following
the twists of the headland to a stile and some steep steps down to a
narrow lane. Turn left for a few yards, then right into a hedged lane past
a farm redolent of country smells. Follow the lane along the ridge, then
right as it drops down to Upton. Head into the village, which is to your
right.

Upton was established as a "satellite" to Headon in Anglo-Saxon times
as woodland clearance created more cultivable land on the parish
boundary. On your left you will find the drive to Hill Top Farm. Pass
the farm, walking on the grass between the crops and a row of

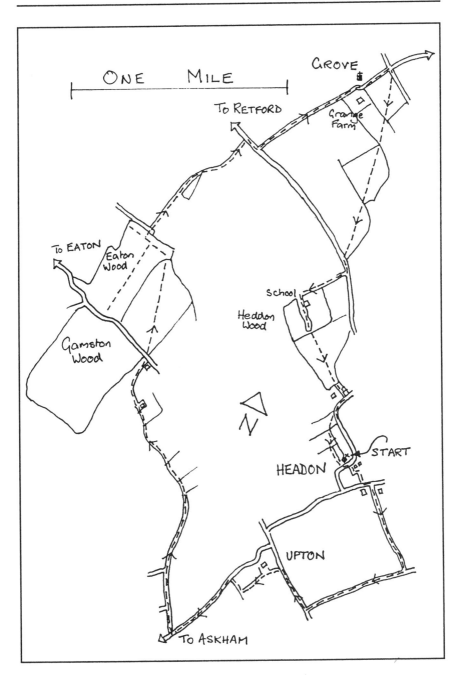

decorative trees, then straight up the mown path at the headland. At the top, turn right along the mown headland to the road. Left turn here and walk for a quarter of a mile as far as Wood Lane on the right. At this point you might consider continuing up the road to Askham, a quiet village with a pleasant pub, the Duke William.

Follow the hedged Wood Lane until it becomes a very green lane indeed and ends in a field. Follow the headland on your left in three fields and pass along the foot of a garden. Here join a track which swings right not far from Gamston Wood to join a road. The next path is opposite and goes corner to corner across an arable field to enter Eaton Wood.

Eaton and Gamston woods were purchased from the Forestry Commission by the Nottinghamshire Wildlife Trust, which manages the woods by coppicing and clearing luxuriant growth to increase the already large stock of wild flowers. They intend to get rid of conifers and return to traditional forest management. There is a public footpath through Eaton Wood but the whole reserve is open to the public. The best time to visit is from mid-April to the end of June. If you come by car please don't park on the verges, as they are rich in flowers.

Follow the North Ride through the wood, passing a track on the left and entering the next junction, which is to the right. At the edge of the wood you join a bridleway, which goes through the gate opposite and continues as a farm track along the edge of a long field, passing a spinney mid-way. At the end, go through the gate, turn right along the road and take the junction left leading to Grove. It was here that the Grove Hunt met in the park of John Carr's mansion, built for the Nevilles in 1762. Now the noble families have gone, the kennels have moved to Serlby, and the house was pulled down in 1951, to be replaced by chicken sheds.

Pass the church and take the hedged lane on the right, or go another 100 yards further to the Garden Centre, where refreshments are available. On entering the hedged lane, turn immediately right again to cross a stile. The path crosses pasture land where the ridge and furrow of mediaeval ploughing can be clearly seen: cross this field diagonally, continue to the gate opposite and go corner to corner again in an arable field. The next field is an enormous meadow in which you climb to the top of the ridge, then head for the left-hand corner.

Cross the stile, turn left along the road for 100 yards and go through the gateway on the right, following the farm track to Schoolhouse Plantation. Between this and Headon Wood is a pleasant glade in which you pass the former schoolhouse, built in 1899 by Mr Harcourt Vernon, squire of the village. At the end of the glade enter a field and follow a row of trees, heading for a handgate at the other end. The path passes through a garden to the road.

Turning to the right, go just around the corner, enter a gateway and follow the path as signposted to a kissing-gate. This is the ideal approach to the short, sturdy tower of Headon church, across grass fields and keeping right of the churchyard to reach the road. It is said that the large doorway in the side of the tower, now filled in, and a matching doorway in the other side, allowed the lord of the manor to enter the church in his coach, from which he followed the service. Turn left to your starting point.

29: DUNHAM & LANEHAM

An easy stroll in the Trent valley following the river towpath and field paths.

Distance: 4.5 miles

Time: 2 hours

Start: Bridge Inn, Dunham, map reference SK 814745

Maps: Pathfinder SK 87/97 (Lincoln), Landranger 121 (Lincoln)

How to Get There:

By Car: Dunham is by the Trent on the A57 Lincoln to Sheffield road

By Bus: Hourly service 39/39a Retford to Tuxford Monday to Saturday, 91

Refreshments: "Ferryboat Inn", Church Laneham, "Butchers Arms", Laneham, "Bridge Inn" and "White Swan", Dunham

Nearest Tourist Information: Retford Tourist Information Centre, Amcott House, 40, Grove Street, Retford (0777 860780)

Start at the Bridge Inn, Dunham. Walk eastwards towards the bridge over the Trent, with a glance at the much-restored church of Saint Giles, notable for the spectacular upper windows in the tower. Near here, before the toll bridge spanned the Trent, the Duke of Portland met William of Orange to escort him to Welbeck, and eventually to the throne of England. Look for a signpost on the left which points along the flood bank. After the first stile you can see your route, which follows the flood bank for a mile and a half to Church Laneham. At the start of this easy stroll, you have a row of willows, most of them formerly pollarded but now allowed to grow naturally.

On reaching Church Laneham, Manor Farm is directly in front of you, and the path is to the right past the orchard to a stile in the corner. This leads into the churchyard, and an opportunity to visit St Peter's church. The 13th century tower of St Peter's has an 11th century Norman hooded doorway, still retaining the original door and hinges.

The path is along the edge of the churchyard with the hedge to your right. Cross a stile, go down to the paddock and left past a row of chalets to reach the road opposite the Ferryboat Inn. To your right is a lane going down to the Trent at the site of the old wharf and of course, it was once possible to cross to Lincolnshire from here by the ferryboat.

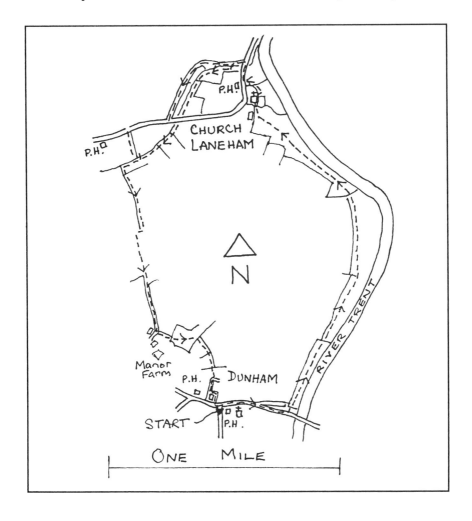

If you have timed the walk well, it might be appropriate to sample the menu at the "Ferryboat" before moving on. To start the return route walk past the church and pub, with a small caravan site on one side and public toilets on the other, as far as a sign on the left which points the way along a wide path. You have a choice here: either follow the track on this side of the Laneham Beck to a road or cross the footbridge on the left, then turn right along the far bank. This is part of the Trent Valley Way, a route devised by Nottinghamshire County Council. It runs along or near the Trent from West Stockwith in the north to Thrumpton in the south of the county.

Whichever you choose you will reach a road. If you choose to follow the wavy arrow signs you have only to cross it and continue along the floodbank. If you followed the track turn left to cross the bridge, then right. A very pleasant path runs along the floodbank beside a willow-shaded stream, with pasture on either side. If bothered by thirst there is a footbridge to the right which leads you into Laneham, where the Butchers Arms can be found to your left.

When faced by a stile it is time to leave the floodbank: turn left along the edge of the field, cross a plank bridge and continue along a clear path at the edge of an arable field. At the end, join a farm track which immediately turns to head toward Manor Farm, Dunham. This lane swings right as it reaches the farm buildings: at this point angle slightly left to cross the fence and follow the edge of a meadow.

On reaching the next gateway the correct line of the footpath is straight on across a farm road and beside a hedge, then left at the corner. However it is easier to turn left along the track which passes close to your destination, a stile and footbridge. Now the route is easy to follow through two grass fields with the hedge on your left, across a narrow strip of arable and along a narrow ginnel. You have now entered "Saint Oswald's Park", a small group of chalets with meticulously-tended gardens. Turn right to leave the estate, and just before the sign-board turn left along a grassy path, then right to skirt an old garden wall.

Reaching the A17, your starting point is to the left, the White Swan is right.

30: CHURCH LANEHAM & COTTAM

A Trentside walk which visits the tiny village of Cottam, passing the inaccessible Torksey castle.

Distance: 6.5 miles

Time: 3.5 hours

Start: Near the Ferryboat Inn at Church Laneham, map reference SK 815768

Maps: Pathfinder SK 87/97 (Lincoln), Landranger 121 (Lincoln)

How to Get There:

By Car: Church Laneham is by the Trent, 2 miles north of Dunham

By Bus: Occasional service 39/39a between Retford and Tuxford

Refreshments: "Moth and Lantern", Cottam, "Ferryboat Inn", Church Laneham

Nearest Tourist Information: Retford Tourist Information Centre, Amcott House, 40 Grove Street, Retford (0777 860780)

/

From the Ferryboat Inn, go north past the riverside caravan site until the road runs beside the river Trent. A grassy sward by the river offers parking for ramblers, fishermen and the less athletically gifted citizens who like to park in front of a nice view and read their Sunday Times. Here a Trent Valley Way signpost invites you to follow the riverside, passing a three-storey Victorian warehouse which has acquired a balcony and a conservatory. Where the riverside path widens out into a meadow, ignore a stile ahead,look for a gap in the hedge left and angle left on to the floodbank, which you follow for a good mile. Just to your left are the eight massive cooling towers of Cottam power station, one of

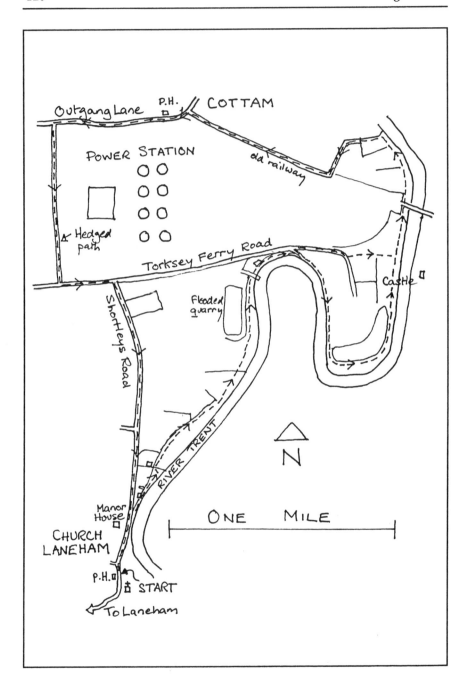

the three riverside coal-fired stations clearly visible at times on this walk.

As you pass the power station, a small gravel pit appears on your left and a gantry straddles the path, taking sand and gravel for transport by barge. Trains of coal waggons circle a black mountain where enormous machines push the coal into some desirable shape, beeping madly.

Soon after passing a small pumping station, you have two options. The first is to stick to the floodbank around a wide loop of the river. This brings you a view of the entrance to Torksey Lock and the Fossdyke Navigation, the canal first created by the Romans to link the Trent and Boston, passing through Lincoln, or Lindum to the original builders. It is the oldest artificial navigation in Britain, dating from 120 A.D. Keep on to the viaduct, a disused railway bridge.

The second option cuts off the loop: turn left to drop down to Torksey Ferry Road, following the lane right until it swings right and climbs over the floodbank. Here there is a stile on your left beside a farm gate, and you can continue to head for the now non-existent ferry. As you reach the Trent bank, you have the best possible view of Torksey castle. Built in Tudor times in stone and brick, it was very soon abandoned and only the river facade remains. Turn left to the viaduct, but do not go through the gate to pass underneath, as the floodbank takes you straight to a stile.

After crossing the disused railway track, half a mile of riverside brings you to a clapper gate. Do not go through, but turn down a grassy lane on the left which crosses a floodbank and returns to a track which seems to follow the original line of the railway. Turn right along this to reach the village of Cottam, then left along the road, passing the Station House with the remains of the station building beyond. The Sheffield to Boston line fell victim to the railway hit-man, Beeching. Just round the corner is the Moth and Lantern (formerly the "Station"), a substantial public house.

Continue along Outgang Lane until, on the left, a hedged path leads down the edge of the power station grounds, crossing two footbridges on the way to Torksey Ferry Road. Turn left, then right into Shortleys Road, a hedged lane which joins the road into Church Laneham and your starting point.

St. Peter's Church Lameham

31: RAMPTON & LEVERTON

The main feature in this walk is the hedged lanes of the Trent valley: access roads to the fields or to a non-existent ferry crossing, surfaced or grassy, they provide vital links for the walker.

Distance: 7.5 miles

Time: 3.5 hours

Start: Rampton church, map reference SK 800786

Map: Pathfinders SK 67/77, 68/78, 87/97, and 88/98, Landranger 121 (Lincoln)

How to Get There:

By Car: Rampton is 6 miles east of Retford via minor roads.

By Bus: Services 91 and 92 hourly from Retford, occasional 39 and 39A between Retford and Tuxford

Refreshments: The "Railway", South Leverton; "Eyre Arms", Rampton.

Nearest Tourist Information: Retford Tourist Information Centre, Amcott House, 40 Grove Street, Retford (0777 860780)

Start at All Saints church, Rampton, taking the lane to the right which becomes a sandy track, Torksey Ferry Road, as it leaves the village. As you get nearer to the cooling towers and enormous chimney of Cottam power station, a signpost on the left indicates a narrow hedged path along the edge of Powergen's property. On reaching Outgang Lane, turn left for 100 yards, then right along a pleasant green lane which crosses the mineral railway line and joins Broad Lane.

Turn right for 200 yards, then left into Southbank Lane. Continue along a field edge and past a tall hedge to join a grassy track on your left. Follow this for three quarters of a mile, with a high hedge of hawthorn

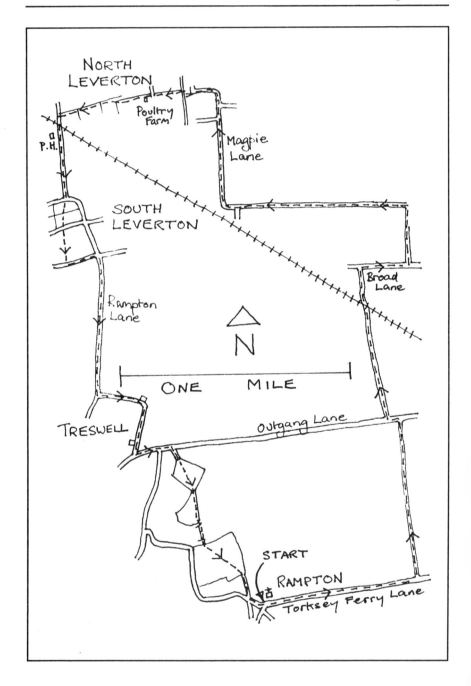

on your left interspersed with ash and field maple. On reaching a lane coming in from the left, go ahead and round the corner, then on along Newings Lane to a double bend. Go round the first corner, but at the second go straight ahead along a field edge to reach the Catchwater Drain. A few yards to your right is a footbridge.

After the bridge the path is straight ahead along a headland, across a lane and past Linsey Poultry Farm, then along the headland again to the corner of the field. Cross the stile and follow the same line, with a hedge on your right, in three meadows to Southgore Lane. Turn left here along the roadside footpath to cross the railway, finding the pub of that name on your right.

Continue to the junction with Mill Lane, cross the stile opposite and follow the well-worn path across two small grass fields to reach the main street of South Leverton. Just opposite is a delightful hedged path between cottage gardens which ends at a back lane. Turn left here, then right at a crossroads into Rampton Lane. After half a mile keep left at a fork and continue to a road, passing two of the "nodding donkeys" which pump oil from Nottinghamshire's small but viable oil-field.

Turn left, pass the end of the Rampton road and enter a short lane on the right after 100 yards. Climb the fence and cross the paddock diagonally. The "castle" seen over the hedge is part of "Sundown Kiddies Adventureland", a mini theme park where children (and parents, of course) can see a variety of animals and disport themselves in an adventure playground.

Climb the stile, pass through an uncultivated area and in the paddock follow the fence on your left to a wrought-iron gate. Cross the driveway leading to Elmwood Lodge to a stile, now following the fence on the right to pass the end of a Dutch barn and enter a large arable field. The path may not be defined here, but aim half-left across it towards the corner. There is a stile and a narrow path to a road. Turn left here to return to your starting-point.

If you have time to visit the church, don't fail to explore the eastern side of the churchyard where a fine 16th century gateway, enriched with armorial panels of the Stanhope and Babington families, is a reminder of the former Tudor Hall. The hall was pulled down in the 18th century.

The more obvious gateway west of the church is the Victorian entrance to a pseudo-Elizabethan hall, which is now divided into flats.

Mock-Tudor gateway

32: TRESWELL ROUND

Treswell Wood, the first reserve to be owned by the Nottinghamshire Wildlife Trust, is at the heart of this walk. It is quite large, 118 acres of ancient woodland and a Site of Special Scientific Interest. Footpaths follow its boundary on two sides.

Distance: 4.5 miles

Time: 2 hours

Start: At the west corner of Treswell Wood, on the road between Grove and Treswell village, map reference SK 758800

Maps: Pathfinders SK 67/77 (Clumber Park) and 68/78 (East Retford North), Landranger 120 (Mansfield & Worksop)

How to Get There:

By Car: The wood is 6 miles east of Retford via minor roads. It is 1.5 miles west of Treswell village.

By Bus: Services 39A, 91, on the Retford/Tuxford route

Refreshments: None en route, visit the "Red Lion" at Treswell before and/or after

Nearest Tourist Information: Retford Tourist Information Centre, Amcott House, 40 Grove Street, Retford (0777 860780)

Start the walk at the west end of Treswell Woods, map reference SK 758800. Walk along the edge of the wood, first on a farm track, then along a field edge. On reaching a narrow tongue of woodland, cross the stream, then a rough wood stile and cross the woodland. The path continues beside the wood, then a substantial parish-boundary hedge, and where the hedge swings left continue across the field, aiming just right of an electricity pole beside North Beck. Continue in the next field to join a farm track beside a small spinney. This leads to a road, where

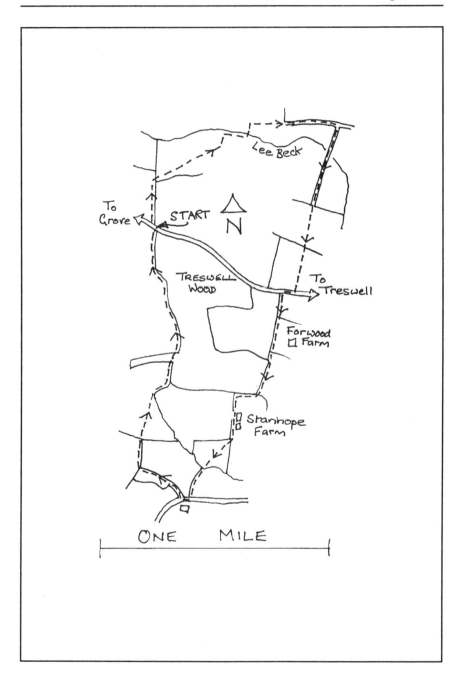

you turn left for a few yards, then left as signposted along a field edge. Just round the corner of the field is a substantial plank bridge and stiles. Continue diagonally right across the arable field to the corner. A gate leads into a lane which leads past the back of Stanhope Farm, then swing left to a gate and on to the edge of Treswell Wood. Turn right beside it, then left through a gate. Walk beside the wood, then straight on to a gate, along the field beside Forwood Farm and along its drive to the road.

Turn right for a few yards, then left as signposted and straight across two fields to join the end of Wood Lane. Follow this to a T-junction, then turn left along Cowsland Road, now only a track beside a hedge. Where this track turns right to Sheds Farm, a bridleway should return you to your starting point. Roughly, it continues to the electricity pole, goes down the field to an overgrown earth bridge, turns right beside the stream to the next bridge, goes up the hill for a hundred yards, angles half-right to the corner of the field and swings left to the road. No traces of it have been found recently, but Nottinghamshire County Council's rights of way section has been notified.

On reaching the road, turn left to your starting point. The wood is normally open to Trust members only, but the Nature Trail is open to the public from 2.00 p.m. to 5.00 p.m. on the second Sunday in the month from April to September inclusive. There is a wide variety of trees, wild flowers and birdlife, and ponds have been created in the wood to provide a home for newts and aquatic plants.

Bibliography

Nottinghamshire, Henry Thorold (Shell)

Nottinghamshire, Nicholas Pevsner (Penguin)

Nottinghamshire Families, Keith Train (Nottinghamshire Local History Society)

Great Houses of Nottinghamshire, L. Jacks (Bradshaw)

Country Houses of Nottinghamshire, Mike Higginbottom (Cromwell Press)

A History of Nottinghamshire Farming, Philip Lyth (Cromwell Press)

A Place to Live: the Nottinghamshire Heritage, Norman Summers (BBC Nottingham)

Industrial Landscapes of the East Midlands, M.Palmer and P.Neaverson (Phillimore)

At Home in Sherwood, Phillip Crowe (Nottingham Building Preservation Trust)

Ancient Bassetlaw, Capt. Roy Peters (North Trent Publishing)

Focus on Bassetlaw, Malcolm Dolby (East Midlands Archaeology #2)

Nicholson's Guide to the Waterways: North-East (British Waterways Board)

The Chesterfield Canal, (Chesterfield Canal Society)

Worksop in Times Past, M.S.Jackson (Countryside Publications)

Illustrated History of Sutton-cum-Lound, Christopher Morton

Headon-cum-Upton - a Short History, J.C.Mosley

Hayton 1762-1914, Rosemary Anderson

Living in East Markham, Ed. Barry Biggs & Brian Hardy (Retford & District Historical & Archaeological Society)

The Town on the Street - Sturton-le-Steeple, Ed. Rev. John Ford

The Old North Road through Babworth, Joan Board

Social History of Toplis' Mill Cuckney, Victoria Millard

Welbeck Abbey, David J.Bradbury Wheel Publications

Our catalogue of over 100 books includes a wide selection of guides to individual towns, plus outdoor activities centred on walking and cycling in the great outdoors throughout England and Wales. This is a recent selection:

PEAK DISTRICT DIARY – Roger Redfern
An evocative book, celebrating the glorious countryside of the Peak District. The book is based on Roger's popular column in *The Guardian* newspaper and is profusely illustrated with stunning photographs. *£6.95*

I REMAIN, YOUR SON JACK – J. C. Morten (edited by Sheila Morten)
A collection of almost 200 letters, as featured on BBC TV, telling the moving story of a young soldier in the First World War. Profusely illustrated with contemporary photographs. *£8.95*

There are many books for outdoor people in our catalogue, including:

RAMBLES IN NORTH WALES
– Roger Redfern

HERITAGE WALKS IN THE PEAK DISTRICT
– Clive Price

EAST CHESHIRE WALKS
– Graham Beech

WEST CHESHIRE WALKS
– Jen Darling

WEST PENNINE WALKS
– Mike Cresswell

NEWARK AND SHERWOOD RAMBLES
– Malcolm McKenzie

RAMBLES AROUND NOTTINGHAM & DERBY
– Keith Taylor

RAMBLES AROUND MANCHESTER
– Mike Cresswell

WESTERN LAKELAND RAMBLES
– Gordon Brown

WELSH WALKS:
Dolgellau and the Cambrian Coast
– Laurence Main and Morag Perrott

WELSH WALKS:
Aberystwyth and District
– Laurence Main and Morag Perrott

– all of these books are currently £6.95 each.